In the southern Highlands of Scotland, the Royal
Scotsman *rumbles across Loch Awe.*

PREVIOUS PAGE: *Dawn breaks over Australia's vast
Nullarbor Plain. For the* Indian Pacific *the end of the line
is still nearly a thousand miles away.*

WORLD'S GREAT
TRAIN JOURNEYS

Adventure, Romance, and
a Kangaroo or Two

NATIONAL
GEOGRAPHIC

WASHINGTON, D.C.

THE EASTERN & ORIENTAL EXPRESS

By Phil Macdonald
Photos by Chris Anderson

THE INDIAN PACIFIC

By Roff Smith
Photos by Kerry Trapnell

Photographs

THE PRIDE OF AFRICA: *Beachfront bathing huts near Cape Town cater to South Africa's sunny side.*

THE SIERRA MADRE EXPRESS: *A spectacular rail journey carries travelers into the heart of Mexico's canyon country.*

THE ROYAL SCOTSMAN: *Small boats lie moored in the harbor of Plockton, a Highland village on the route of the* Scotsman.

THE EASTERN & ORIENTAL EXPRESS: *Bangkok's rambunctious Chinatown is one of the busiest areas of this sprawling, clamorous city.*

THE INDIAN PACIFIC: *Road sign on the lonely Eyre Highway warns motorists of wild camels, wombats, and kangaroos in the deserts ahead.*

THE PRIDE OF AFRICA

By Douglas
Bennett Lee

Photos by
Tino Soriano

There's a certain hushed music
on a railroad platform in the hour
before a train's leaving,

an echoing background symphony of bustle and screech, sighing steam, peals of brakes, clashes of iron cars coupling and uncoupling under barn-high tin roofs. It's a song of travel, of escape from stations and cities and time as we usually know it…of going, from wherever you are to an eternal elsewhere, promising space and distance, open skies, places and people, and all things new.

There's a certain hazy light you may recognize, conjuring train stations from when you were young—chiaroscuro sun-shafts slanting from smoky skylights through lofty rafters where pigeons fly.

You may remember smells: diesel smoke, tar, and hot metal.

And on Platform 23 of South Africa's Cape Town Station, on a Monday morning that has a Saturday feel to it, you may experience a sense of déjà vu from a time you never knew but somehow seem to remember, triggered by scents of travel from an earlier era—perfumes and champagne and well-tooled leather luggage—as passengers gather to take a ride through Africa on the railway that bills its trains, without blinking, as "the Most Luxurious in the World."

It's a long, elegant, royal green beast breathing in its sleep on the track beside us—resting, gathering its strength for a journey of nearly a thousand miles. It will be a trip through history as well as distance, from South Africa's Mother City to its hinterlands, past farmlands, vineyards, deserts, and diamond mines to Johannesburg, the City of Gold, and on to Pretoria, its old-shoe sister city and the nation's administrative capital.

That's the first thousand miles. After a night off the train in Pretoria,

PRECEDING PAGES: *The moody backdrop of Table Mountain sets a dramatic stage as Cape Town comes alight for the evening. South Africa's oldest city and port is also a jumping-off point for the luxurious rolling adventure-on-wheels known as the* Pride of Africa.

we'll re-embark for the northern mountains, the Drakensberg, and beyond them the Lowveld, the country's chief game-ranching district adjoining Mozambique and Kruger National Park, where the wild frontier lingered into living memory, and animals still have right-of-way.

All told we'll spend four nights aboard, then cap it off by flying on to

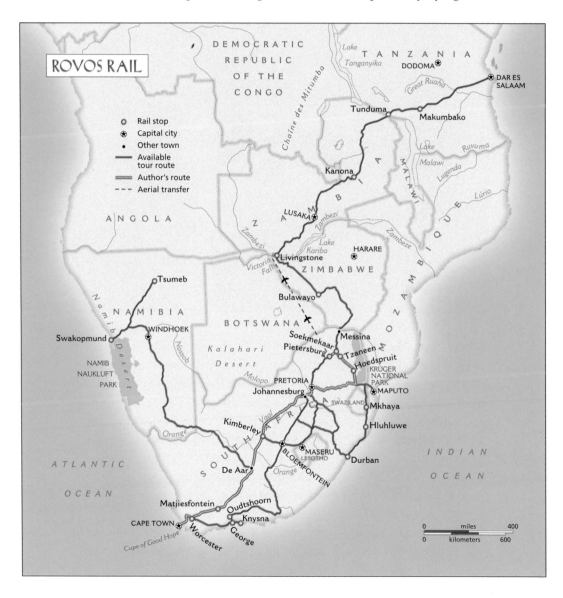

Zimbabwe's first-ranked resort, Victoria Falls, in a "vintage aircraft"—not a phrase to encourage the nervous flyer, but actually a meticulously cared for DC-4, built in 1946, a proud member of a fleet of senior airplanes still flying charters around southern Africa in active old age.

All the while we'll be wrapped in a cocoon of carefully constructed opulence harking back to the age of empire, when Victorian and Edwardian ladies and officers rode the rails of a young British colony rich with diamonds and gold. It's an experience not without contradictions, taking a luxury train through a country that combines elements of the First World and

developing nations living cheek by envious jowl. In a certain sense the railway's mirror-shiny, dark green carriages reflect not only the passing countryside, but also the charms and dichotomies, and the sometimes jarring realities, of life in the 21st-century Rainbow Nation.

Like many improbable success stories, Rovos Rail is the embodiment of one man's vision, enthusiasm, and sense of fun—a toy about as big as a grown-up's toy can get. It's the brainchild, pet, and full-time avocation of Rohan Vos, a restless, self-made auto parts entrepreneur who in 1986 listened to his heart over his financial instincts and turned his business acumen from road to rails.

His conversion came when he tried to hire South African Railways to pull a private train taking his family and friends on an adventure outing.

Old wood and old-worldly lamplight warm a once derelict dining car
meticulously restored to its original glory by Rohan Vos, owner and
namesake of Rovos Rail. Calling his trains "the Most Luxurious in
the World," he accentuates historical charm and authenticity.

The high price he was quoted offended his better business principles…and piqued his interest.

"For that amount," he figured, "I could build my own train!"

So he did.

In a midlife switch of career tracks, he combined his first and last names into the eponymous Rovos Rail and cast his fate to the singing trestles—though not without a long look up the tracks. He rode and investigated luxury trains all over the world, and in his travels came to recognize in South Africa's rich railroad heritage the subcontinent's answer to such internationally well known belles as Europe's *Orient Express*, North America's *Canadian*, and the United Kingdom's *Flying Scotsman*.

South Africa's own *Blue Train* was already famous among well-heeled travelers and railroad buffs, setting standards of excellence since 1946 aboard modern luxury cars running between Cape Town and Pretoria. Rohan decided to set his railway apart with a polished patina of historical luster.

Standing derelict in forgotten rail yards or still toiling along backwater side lines and narrow mountain trestles in odd corners of the country were cars and engines, venerable survivors from an era that ended when the last working steam engine retired in 1991. Most of the locomotives he found were already in the hands of scrap-metal dealers. Rohan rescued them and applied an affinity for things mechanical to the new challenge of bringing South African steam travel back to life. In the process he built his own empire—today Rovos Rail is the world's largest privately owned luxury railroad, an achievement of questionable financial security, but robust emotional reward.

"At age 40," Rohan is wont to say, "I was well off. Now I'm broke. But boy, do I have a great train set!"

The fleet he commands numbers five working locomotives (each named after a family member, the sort of perk that comes with owning your own railroad); sixty or more sleeper coaches, most renovated into plush, teak-paneled roomettes complete with writing tables, floor-to-ceiling lockers, and en suite bathrooms with showers (the most spacious "Royal" suites add a full-size old-fashioned bathtub); six period-piece dining cars, the oldest replete with elaborately carved wooden pillars and sconces; and a half-dozen fashionably cozy lounge cars lined with windows that open to let breezes blow past passengers talking, reading, or dozing on overstuffed couches and armchairs.

As a last thought on every train comes a feature many passengers prize most: an open-air platform at the rear of a comfortably furnished observation and bar car, from which to watch the world go past your elbow.

Rohan oversees a web of routes that takes in several of South Africa's

Flourishes of tribal dress distinguish young performers of the musical group Buka Afrika on Cape Town's tourist-friendly waterfront. Long a melting pot of cultures and races, Cape Town has a history of encouraging artists and the arts, from traditional to nouveau.

FOLLOWING PAGES:
Life wears vivid Mediterranean hues in a trendy Cape Town neighborhood. Ocean airs, nearby beaches, and a California climate aid Cape-tonians in dedicated pursuit of a lifestyle with less emphasis on stress than on appreciating their city's gifts.

most celebrated scenic and historic regions, then carries on past the country's borders. One excursion reaches to Namibia's deserts and the Atlantic coast, another to Mozambique's tropical shores. The most ambitious is an African odyssey that winds from South Africa through Zimbabwe, Zambia, and Tanzania to the Indian Ocean at Dar es Salaam, a journey of 13 days and 3,800 miles.

The route we've booked holds plenty to catch my imagination. No place is more fitting to start an exploration of South Africa than Cape Town, and no place more meet to stay than the sprawling pink castle of the Mount Nelson Hotel. It's an institution still going strong from the century before last, a five-star grand dame built in the 1890s at the high tide of the British Empire, coincidentally with the beginnings of modern South Africa and the railroads that bound the young country together.

Here leading families of South Africa's oldest and most cosmopolitan city still meet for high tea, or to celebrate anniversaries under the dining room's soaring mural of the Dutch settlement at its bucolic 17th-century beginnings. From the high-ceilinged, antique-decorated bedrooms to the bust of Lord Adm. Horatio Nelson in the dark-paneled bar, old times are not forgotten.

Cape Town is one of the world's great maritime cities, for centuries the hinge between sea-lanes that girdle the globe and the endless Africa beyond the coastal mountains. The harbor at night, ringed by yellow lamps and studded with vessels at anchor lighted like jeweled birds, can tug at a traveler's heartstrings, even if you have trains on your mind.

But the dominant, magical presence that lends Cape Town its never-never land air is Table Mountain, rising from sea level to 3,566 feet, crouched like a cloud-capped sphinx looking out to the Southern Ocean past the city draped over its paws. All day the sandstone face casts a shifting interplay of light and shadow, a tapestry of mingled gray rock and olive vegetation that changes hour by hour. At night powerful floodlights keep the mountain awake, painting the rippling curtain of rock like a floating battlement above the city. My wife, Sigrid, and I gaze up at it from the window of our room in the grand old hotel before closing our eyes—a vision to make wishes on.

The mountain still beckons by daylight, its aerial cableway leading to one of the world's great views over what Sir Francis Drake called "the fairest Cape we saw in the whole circumference of the earth." But our business now has to do with leaving.

Rovos Rail's hospitality manages to be both low-key and impeccable, from the moment attendants meet you curbside at the station. The organization is a marriage of enthusiasm and engineering, vision and obsession. Rohan is famous—some staff might say notorious—for his attention to detail. Every wooden fitting and brass screw in every cabin has been set in place by himself or a picked handful of trusted artisans. Each item on the menu has met his approval. As often as not, he's on the platform in Cape Town to wish his guests bon voyage. But today his representative is train manager Bruce Parkinson, a combination host, guide, maître d', and problem solver.

"Yes," he admits, "my grandmother calls me a conductor."

"This is a train to enjoy," he tells our newly assembled group of 32 passengers as we sip champagne and fresh-squeezed orange juice. "We do ask that you dress for dinner. It needn't be formal—jacket and tie are acceptable—although tuxedos are appreciated."

Sigrid and I glance covertly at our fellow travelers, who are covertly glancing at each other and us. We're heartened to observe that few resemble the models we've studied in the Rovos Rail brochures, dauntingly elegant couples resplendent in evening wear in the lamp-lit dining salon, or willowy young things draped oh-so-casually in the observation car.

What we see could be any group in any airport lounge, about to be called for the better seats on an intercontinental flight: a multiaged bunch relaxed in slacks and windbreakers, safari jackets, designer jeans.

South Africa's leading tourist attraction, Cape Town's Victoria and
Albert Waterfront showcases restaurants, bars, discos, and boutiques
beside a gentrified harbor. Beyond it Table Mountain, the nation's
most recognizable landmark, wears its distinctive tablecloth of cloud.

Dining car attendant Bester Joubert oversees immaculate presentation of gourmet meals and top South African wines. Formal wear is suggested for dinner, when the bill of fare runs to game meats, seafood from South African waters, and celebrated local beef and lamb.

The roots of viticulture reach nearly to the beginnings of South
Africa's European history. Founded soon after Dutch settlers arrived
at the Cape of Good Hope in 1652, gracious 17th-century vineyards
still prosper, to growing international recognition.

Children of the Great Karoo region play by the train at historic Matjiesfontein Station, built in the late 1800s when British railroads reached across the arid inland plateau to link Cape Town with gold and diamond bonanzas farther north. Re-creating Edwardian-era opulence, Rovos Rail also affords passengers a cross-section, eye-level view of South Africa.

There's one thing all of us are wearing, as a trio of strolling musicians strikes up a gypsy air and we walk to our assigned cabins and meet the car attendants who will be on call 24 hours a day. It's a look of expectation for the main actor that's drawn us all here—the train that stands on the track beside us, engine humming, awaiting a whistle to take us to Africa.

THE RHYTHM OF RAILS SOUNDS DEEP IN THE HISTORY OF MY SOUTHERN FAMILY, THE legacy of a grandfather, great-grandfather, and several great-uncles who worked for the timber-company railroads of Mississippi and Louisiana. Some of my father's earliest memories are of trains trundling past the front doors of company houses in the evanescent lumber towns that sprang up in the piney woods where my grandfather drove a steam locomotive. When, some 50 years later, my father had his choice of offices in a Pittsburgh skyscraper, he chose the one with the best view of the B & O switching yards.

I have my own memories of faraway train whistles, and horns and bells and clicking trestles in many countries and years. So my pulse stirs at the familiar but ever new lurch as the *Pride of Africa* starts out of Cape Town Station.

The place to be is on the open observation platform, in company with other passengers effervescent with departure and bubbling wines. The guest roster represents five continents and a wide gamut of characters, from quietly retired couples to middle-aged adventurers to well-traveled and exuberant twentysomethings. Jamaican businessman and bon vivant Horace Bogues is still exhilarated from a close encounter of a few months before, on a guided dive with great white sharks in open ocean off Belize.

"You could reach out and touch them," he exults. "I can't wait to do it again!"

British businessman Bob is taking a holiday from a holiday of sorts, crewing on a round-the-world sailboat race. He's just completed the leg from Rio de Janeiro to Cape Town. A week or so ago he was riding 60-foot seas in the roaring forties. Now he's with his wife, Eileen, who's joined him for this gently rocking land-bound interlude. Bob wears one diamond earring and a private smile that never seems to leave his face.

Everyone has his or her reasons for being here, and every one is different. Allison is taking a break from making natural history films in Bristol, England, to treat her mother to an African journey for a milestone birthday. Law partners Meena and Helen are temporarily forgetting the domestic legal cases they handle in London. Tim, Paul, and Cindy are brothers and a sister in their 20s from Queens, New York, a tight trio making an African trip as a family present, in part to help deal with their grief at another sibling's death.

Over the next days and nights we will pass each other countless times in the swaying corridors, join each other for lunches and dinners, watch sunsets from the observation balcony, sit up at the chrome-and-mahogany bar telling stories later than we should—all parts of the magic of a mode of travel largely lost to our times. No airplane ride has ever left me with a pocketful of cards of newly made friends.

Our locomotive is a modern electric engine—Rohan's reconstructed old masters are saved for short hauls or special trips—and there's no steam whistle blowing or smokestack puffing. But Cape Town's sweep of mountains, city, and sea supplies the romance as we watch its clustered skyscrapers grow smaller.

Horace raises a glass. "Well, here's to Table Mountain—and there she goes."

The flat-topped peak is wearing a white sheet of cloud spilling over its brows, known as "the Tablecloth." Visible for 30 miles and more at sea, the mountain has greeted mariners since Bartolomeu Dias led Portuguese caravels round the Cape in 1487. For half a millennium it's been the signpost where Africa meets the world, and there is something quieting about watching it dwindle.

We pass nondescript suburbs and industrial parks, then a sudden apparition, the incongruous faux-Disney ramparts of an enormous amusement park. Just offshore, I know, blocked from our view by wealthy seaside development, lies Robben Island, where Nelson Mandela overcame his 28-year imprisonment to lead his nation out of the greater captivity of apartheid.

Soon we are surrounded by a slum of world-class order. Even on this journey, or perhaps especially on this one, there's no forgetting the peaks and valleys of wealth and poverty that pocket South Africa's social landscape.

A maze of irregular houses and treeless yards stretches out of sight on either side of the tracks. Some buildings are made of cinder block, others of scrap wood, corrugated tin, flattened aluminum cans, plastic bags. Skinny dogs trot past children playing in puddles on potholed red-clay streets. A haze of wood and coal smoke rises from countless chimneys and open fires. Few men or women lift their faces as we pass above them on the elevated embankment. Those who do, do not smile.

Glen Hall, the train's steward and bartender, has been making frequent rounds of the observation car to freshen glasses, but now he steps onto the balcony with a piece of advice for those of us riding alfresco.

"I just need to mention that there've been rocks thrown by children as we've passed through this area. So be aware, and if something should happen, come inside."

When has something happened, I ask?

"There were windows broken on the run in," he replies.

No seat quite like it, the open-air rear platform beckons guests at all hours to a diorama of South Africa's changing landscapes. Leaving the Karoo, the Pride of Africa *passes through green farmlands to Kimberley, the city made by diamonds. Here the world's biggest handmade excavation (opposite), 705 feet deep, sits at the city's center, where 19th-century diggers hauled away fortunes, but left behind the foundations of the world's leading diamond industry.*

FOLLOWING PAGES: *The sibilant voice of steam sounds once again as the locomotive* Bianca *takes to the rails. Built in 1938 and rescued from early retirement by Rohan, it's one of five in his fleet, decades after nearly all other South African rail traffic turned to diesel and electricity.*

Fortunately for Glen, he wasn't the steward on duty when a well-publicized incident occurred a year or so before. Some passengers on the rear balcony had beckoned to a passerby on the platform while the train was stopped at a station near Pretoria.

"They asked some chap if they could take his picture," Rohan told me

in an interview. "This fellow obliged and walked over to them, and they took his picture. He then told them he'd like their cameras, and climbed up onto the train to collect them."

South Africa suffers one of the world's highest violent-crime rates, and few people born and bred here would wave their valuables in a public place. The overseas visitors paid for their naiveté with their cameras, then fled into the observation car. The robber followed them inside. The steward on duty saw what was happening and came out from behind the bar gripping a champagne bottle by the neck. The intruder then produced a gun, and the barman fell to the floor just as a shot was fired.

"I think the chap may only have meant to fire a warning shot into the floor," Rohan said, "but the steward was hit in the leg. Not very seri-

Cozy comfort ensconced in Edwardian elegance is the hallmark of sleeper carriages Rohan has renovated as period pieces. Attendant Yvonne Meyer makes up a double bed in a suite that typically includes a desk, closets, and bathroom with glass-booth shower.

ously, thankfully, and the chap turned and ran.

"This is the only serious incident we've had in 15 years," Rohan is quick to point out. He changed itineraries to avoid stops at potential trouble spots. South Africans have a long history of adjusting to evils not otherwise easily remedied.

Amid the township's drab bleakness, I begin to see brighter details. Rows of neatly set, multicolored bottles outline clean-swept front yards. Painted tires serve as flowerpots. Well-tended vegetable gardens and patches of corn thrive behind one-room houses. Most men and women, I notice, are well dressed despite unkempt surroundings, more dignified than their environment. Then a group of children stop their play at a game of their own devising, on and around an abandoned hut, and look up at us and wave and yell. They laugh when we wave back, and a few run after us. They are still laughing and waving, shouting after us, when they disappear, along with Cape Town, around a final bend.

⥊⬦⥋

THROUGH AN ECHOING TUNNEL AND OVER A LOW PASS WE ENTER A LAND OF MILK and honey—or perhaps, wine and money. This is South Africa's Empire of the Grape, famous for labels that can hold their heads up in the most distinguished international company.

The names of the estates are Dutch and French, going back to Huguenot settlers who brought viticulture from the Old Country in the 1680s. The soils and sunny Mediterranean climate took the new arrivals to their earthy breast, and vines and vintners prospered. The earliest families still own vast holdings, and theirs are the names we see on the wine list when we follow the chimes to the dining car. Food and drink are included in the ticket, so there's no reason to waste away. Bruce recommends a Klein Constantia Rhine Riesling with the warm Mediterranean salad, then a red Rustenberg Stellenbosch with the veal loin medallions, or if preferred the cheese-filled gnocchi, in which case he suggests another white.

Sigrid will have the sparkling Cap Classique Krone Borealis, thank you. She's a South African girl who knows her country's wines, and also, I've noticed, what she likes.

"It's made by the same method as French champagne," she tells me, "and I think it's just as good. They just can't call it champagne."

Every item on the menu is a South African product, a point of which Rohan is proud. Ironically, Sigrid is the only South African passenger. Rovos Rail's prices are competitive by dollar standards, but expensive for South Africans paying in rand. If not for the train staff, South Africans of Afrikaner,

An elephant's love is hard to ignore, as gamekeeper Flippie already knows about Jabulani, the biggest and fastest growing ward at Hoedspruit Research and Breeding Centre for Endangered Species, located within the Kapama Private Game Reserve. A regular stop on Rovos Rail's Lowveld route, the center works with endangered African species and orphaned or disabled individuals.

PRECEDING PAGES: *Rugged profiles of the Hex River Mountains rise over a valley lush with orchards and vineyards in the Cape region. Farther north another range, the Drakensberg, marks the border of the Lowveld, South Africa's prime game country, where parks and private ranches preserve wildlife and tended wilderness.*

British, and African tribal backgrounds, she might have felt like a foreigner in her own land.

The wines are good by any continental tastes. Good enough to excuse the claims on a certificate we found waiting for us in the cabin when we arrived, along with fresh flowers and a welcoming basket of chocolate and fruit, entitled the Golden Age of Luxury Travel (suitable for framing). Rohan must have had fun composing it (though I suspect he believes it, too):

> *Be it known that the prerogative to ride on board the Greatest Train on Earth has been exercised by Mr. & Mrs. Lee. By this action, a persistent thirst has been slaked at the rail-bound water hole…while…culinary delights have been savored…in the restaurant car Shangani.*

The dining car is an aesthetic experience in itself. Built in 1924 and restored by Rohan, Coach 195 Shangani is named for the Shangaan, one of South Africa's major tribes, but harks back to purely European ancestry. Its teak pillars and arches frame tables with the look and feel of an elite restaurant in belle epoque Paris. The warm red wood, crisp white linen and fine china, sparkling crystal and glinting silver all render a spell that entices us to linger at table, especially when a sweet Weisser Riesling Noble Late Harvest accompanies the honey nougatine parfait dessert, and a 15-year-old South African port is proffered with aged cheeses.

The estates whose vintages we're sampling are passing outside our windows as we dine. A picture-book landscape of neatly laid vineyards and orchards and evergreen windbreaks takes on heroic dimensions as we move beneath the craggy peaks of the Hex River Valley. Here mountains worthy of John Ford's cinematic American West tower over a valley out of Bruegel's idyllic Low Country paintings, a tranquil and domesticated farmscape where distant figures work waist-high in vines, a cart horse trots along a dusty road, and white mansions in the thatch-roofed Cape Dutch style gaze out over their domains from plantings of old trees.

The last line of Rohan's certificate reads, …*such person has been lulled to sleep in the cozy confines of a luxurious suite.*

Luxurious sleep is what Sigrid and I want after our explorations in vinous geography. The berths on Rovos Rail are proper beds, not fold-up bunks, and ready for napping, for which we are grateful. Ours is a double across one end of the cabin. We close the wooden shutters and pull the heavy shades, and for the first but not the last time lie down to the steady, soothing rhythm of rails meeting wheels beneath our heads.

I wake to find Sigrid gazing out the pillow-level window at a changed world. Gone the harvest land of plenty. Flat brush stretches to the horizon, purple and long-shadowed by a late sun. Barbed wire fences run alongside us, then veer off. A farmstead stands alone in mid-distance, windmill turning, a cluster of sheltering trees shaped by wind into a teardrop.

"The Karoo," Sigrid says.

The Great Karoo is South Africa's answer to Australia's outback, an ancient lake bed rich in fossils, sheep, and little else that meets the eye. The numberless herds of springbok that early explorers encountered here are long gone to hunters' guns. Yet like many flat, homely places, the Karoo softens and deepens with the sun's late rays until it takes on an oil-paint patina, and the ghosts of vanished herds lope alongside us in our half-dreams as the shadows stretch away.

The sun has set when we glide into the historic hamlet of Matjies-fontein, a rail-side attraction that grew around a dining canteen built for train passengers in the late 1880s, before the Cape to Kimberley rail-line masters thought of dining cars. A poster from the time advertises that lavatory facilities are available at all meal stops, a first order of business for travelers of any era.

Renovated Victorian shops, a pub, and the fanciful, turreted, hundred-year-old Lord Milner Hotel enjoyed a fleeting period as an international destination in the great age of train travel. Now most visitors reach the museum village by car. But there's a rightness in stepping onto the platform from the long, panting train in a warm dusk, just as empire-builder Cecil Rhodes did in the 1880s when stopping to commune with Olive Schreiner, South Africa's first woman novelist and a feminist who was also anti-imperialist and, later, antiapartheid. She was also a romantic, who found tranquillity at Matjies-fontein, yet who, paradoxically, until the looming Boer War drove them apart, had for a brief time the power to touch Rhodes's domineering heart.

The antique storefronts and tall blue gum trees rustling in the desert breeze lend an air of grandeur to the scene, incongruously lit by London street lamps imported in the town's heyday. But after a brief visit we're back on board and headed for the dining car, while the *Pride of Africa* carries us north into the night.

Morning finds the Karoo still with us, but gradually the land takes on a cultivated, midwestern look with fields of commercial flowers, swelling grasslands, and fresh-tilled fields. After a lunch of *bobotie*, a traditional Afrikaner curry-flavored casserole, we enter Kimberley, the city that diamonds built.

"The railway is my arm and the telegraph my voice," Rhodes said as he dreamed of an empire and a railroad under British dominion running from Cape Town to Cairo, starting with the route we're following. He might have added that diamond mines were his wallet. South Africa's deposits of diamonds and gold are among the greatest in the world, and the Boer War

*"Africa After Hours" is a show not seen by every visitor to the bush,
as Africa's wild country is called. Private game ranches extend the
privilege of night drives in some of Africa's richest game country to
Rovos Rail passengers who make the Pretoria to Durban safari trip
and visit the resorts as a treat on their itineraries.*

In constant vigil for Africa's "Big Five"—lion, leopard, rhino, Cape buffalo, and elephant—a game scout scours the bush while a client does the same from the back of a roofless safari vehicle. Rohan promotes a number of specialty-theme "Train Safaris," including one that visits several of South Africa's top reserves.

FOLLOWING PAGES: *Away from the eyes of the African night but open to the stars, Rovos guests dine by firelight at a game ranch's* boma, *usually reserved for the ranch's clients. Noted for its sumptuous decor and cuisine, the lodge relaxes its style a bit in the boma with a traditional South African cookout, called a* braai.

(which Rhodes did all in his power to precipitate) secured both for the British Empire. He died soon after the war ended, and the Trans-Africa railroad was never achieved. But the nation he welded biting and kicking together took the shape South Africa has today.

A reconstructed museum village showcases carriages, train gear, and

items of daily life from Kimberley's early days in the late 1800s, along with the first diamond ever officially recorded in South Africa—the Eureka, a sparkling 10.73 carats. But the most breathtaking monument to the era's rapacity is an enormous excavation that was South Africa's first and greatest diamond digging. Known as the Big Hole, it's Earth's largest hand-dug pit, 705 feet deep, partly filled with green water, and a mile in circumference. It started off, before it was revealed in 1871 to be the tip of an ancient volcanic pipe of diamond-rich rock, as a small hill.

Birds fly to roosts on its far side, tiny with distance. Every ounce of dirt, ore, and diamonds was dug and hauled out by human exertion. Out of countless thousands of prospectors from all over the world, a few got rich, many died, and more went bust. Rhodes founded a financial empire that bought

Close-knit camaraderie of fellow travelers finds convivial spirits in the observation car, which beckons passengers with a bar, the rear-platform open-air balcony (past the sliding glass doors)—and a multinational after-dinner card game between new friends.

him his own colony, Rhodesia, and gave rise to De Beers Consolidated Mines, today's 600-pound gorilla of the diamond business, which still makes Kimberley its headquarters—just the way Rhodes would have liked it.

Back in Rohan Vos's empire, we sit down to a meal Rhodes might have enjoyed: Smoked salmon, roast leg of Karoo lamb (its distinctive flavor imparted by the Karoo's succulent browse), and traditional Cape brandy pudding, a hearty and heartwarming dessert that encourages a group of us to bring our coffees to the open balcony. Though we've only been aboard two days and nights, it seems we've known each other longer, and there's a certain wistful feel about tomorrow's stop in Pretoria, where some of us will be leaving.

"I've never been so stressed out as this last year at work," says a Scotsman named Taffy, sipping his national stress reliever, "to the point where it was affecting my health. But after a couple of days on the train, I realized, it doesn't matter. Life's too short. Look at all this!" He gestures at the sleeping world moving by under an arching sky of moon. "How beautiful it is, how big it is...and I think, why can't you make your thinking that way?"

We rattle through the darkness on our bright-lit, rushing ship, alone as if at sea, insulated from care for this brief time by speed and company, and the alchemy of motion.

⋙⋘

LIKE GEOMETRIC ANT HEAPS, SLAG HILLS OF GOLD-ORE TAILINGS FORM UNNATURAL ranges as we near Johannesburg, indicating the warren of mines beneath them. Some shafts reach more than two miles into Earth's crust, the deepest in the world, and they've made Johannesburg Africa's richest city, the hustling New York of the southern subcontinent. But the *Pride of Africa* slides through the metropolis toward a quieter destination: The tidy, serene, scrubbed brick station that is the heart of Rovos Rail, a once derelict marshaling yard outside Pretoria that Rohan has made his headquarters and Shangri-la.

He's waiting at Capital Park's airy, colonial-style lounge to meet us, among wicker furniture and fresh flowers and paintings of trains, a tall, personable man who greets every passenger and cocks his head to listen. Manager Bruce Parkinson has told me it's not unusual for Rohan to help guests with their luggage, and every once in a while he's offered a tip.

Upstairs in his office, he overlooks his fiefdom with fond satisfaction.

"Everybody's played with toy trains," he says. "At a little distance, like we are here, you're looking down on a train set. The fact that it's big doesn't mean you can't still put your hand out and move them around."

Beside watercolors of locomotives *Brenda*, named after his oldest

Noble beak of a tough old bird points north
toward Zimbabwe and Victoria Falls, where the
scrupulously maintained DC-3 will deliver
Rovos Rail's passengers on the last leg of their
journey to a scenic wonder of the world.

FOLLOWING PAGES: A thundering curtain of
water a mile long, Victoria Falls has been
sought out by travelers since David Livingstone
viewed it in 1855, yet still retains its
powers of inspiration.

Over the rainbow and the crest of Vic Falls lies Zambia, on the far shore of the Zambezi River. On the Zimbabwean side, tough economic and political times can't keep citizens from enjoying their country's greatest international symbol and tourist magnet, where a teacher photographs his students on a school outing.

daughter, and *Tiffany*, for his youngest, a map on the wall shows all the routes his trains take. What do they add up to, I wonder.

Rohan stops and thinks. "Twenty-one thousand kilometers [13,000 miles]," he says. "That's kilometers of different track."

His fertile businessman's imagination has spawned a number of train safaris, specialty excursions to top-ranked golf resorts or game-viewing ranches, for instance, or hunting estates for prime game bird shooting. A third of his passengers are repeat customers, and more than half the patrons on the annual cross-continental marathon from Cape Town to Dar es Salaam have traveled on Rovos before. Rohan usually goes along on those trips, lending his convivial presence as host, troubleshooting through any sticking points along the Third World route, and not infrequently tending bar in the observation car.

"I'm a restless sort," he says. "One minute I'm down with my screwdriver putting in a bathroom fitting, then I'm shouting at the engineer, then I'm drinking with my friends and guests.

"The whole thing revolves around having fun. I'm having fun, most certainly. Building things and building up old things is one of my greater pleasures. A train is animate, it's not a dead thing, it moves. Every coach has its own history, its own creak and bang and crash.

"These trains of mine, I like to think, have a soul."

In the vast, shadowy locomotive sheds, once home to more than a hundred engines, I find myself communing with the soul of Rohan's oldest locomotive, *Tiffany*, built in 1893 when my grandfather was three years old, as it sits alone, fires newly lit to build up steam. Standing in the engineer's place at the controls, picturing the stoker shoveling coal as the Mississippi woods rushed past, feeling the waft of flames that lick along the lip of the firebox, touching the shiny brass throttle and itching to pull the steam whistle, I feel in my solar plexus a tingle my grandfather must have known.

Next morning *Tiffany* prances past, frisky as a filly, and toots her whistle at us as we gather on Capital Park's veranda to reboard. There are new faces, and though we can't help but feel the superiority of old hands, we're soon meeting new fellow travelers from Germany, Finland, Canada, and Russia, as well as Britons, Americans, and one couple who list their home as not the United Kingdom, but Scotland.

Brenda pulls us out of the station and a few miles up the track, chuffing aromatic steam and smoke. From the rear balcony I look back to see Rohan standing on the platform gazing after us, looking as if he wishes he were aboard. We soon switch to a diesel locomotive powerful enough to haul us up and down the grades ahead. After a lunch of smoked-duck salad and ostrich medallions, we escape the twin cities' sprawling industrial exurbs for the golden rolling grasslands that typify the Highveld, the 6,000-

foot-elevation High Plains of South Africa. Only occasional massive smoke-stacks of power plants and smelters on the horizon remind us we're traveling over untold mineral wealth.

By late afternoon we're in the red-rock canyons of the Drakensberg, and after sunset we begin the descent down their eastern escarpment, a drop of more than 2,000 feet to the subtropical Lowveld. Well into the 20th century this was the border of the frontier, where hunters, explorers, and traders proceeded at risk of wild animals and hostile Africans, and even more of the *Anopheles* mosquito and the malaria protozoan it bears to this day. Only modern malaria prophylactics allowed the region to be settled by farmers and game ranchers, and the endemic disease makes it strongly advisable for Rovos Rail passengers to take some form of antimalarial medication on this trip, as Sigrid and I are doing.

The steepest stretch traverses eight and a half miles of tunnels and switchbacks between towns just three and a half miles apart as the crow flies. But first the train pauses high up in a valley where we can see a busy highway below, the main road from Johannesburg. It's one Sigrid and I have driven often, looking up at the train tracks winding along riverbanks and mountainsides. There's a childlike pleasure in looking down, for once, on the streams of auto lights, and it prompts Sigrid to remember her childhood, when she and her sister, Britt, took trains between boarding school in Johannesburg and homes in the Lowveld and Mozambique.

"This is the same track we took back then," she recalls, "before there was a highway. We loved it going home. Hated going back to school. Mind you, we didn't see all that much scenery. We'd get on in the afternoon, then after supper it was straight to bed, and when we woke up, we'd be in Mozambique."

Next morning finds us as near to Mozambique as this trip will take us, on the borders of Kruger National Park. We drink in the winelike air of the Lowveld, heady with humidity and the sagelike scent of its spiky, feather-leaved acacia woodlands. Little except flat, near-sea-level plain lies between us and the Indian Ocean a hundred miles away. Its moisture brings puffy, flat-bottomed, low-flying cumulus sailing like a fleet of white ships across the sky. Our sense of the rightness of the world is jarred as we slow to approach the Klaserie siding, where we'll stop to visit a game-breeding ranch. Flat cars, box cars, and tank cars lie jumbled beside the tracks like broken toys stacked or scattered at random, carelessly flung amid great raw gouges plowed into the soil.

A further tragic note sounds when we learn that a woman who was to be our driver at the Kapama Private Game Reserve was killed in a head-on collision minutes before we arrived. Kapama's staff bravely soldiers on in

Miles and miles of Africa take myriad shapes as Rohan Vos's magic carpets of steel carry the lucky few through time as well as space. Billed as a luxury experience, his trips take on a deeper meaning for some, drawing on the nostalgia of an older time while serving up the ever new feast of Africa today.

the face of their shock, showing us the cheetahs, lions, and other wild cats they rescue and raise at the Hoedspruit Research and Breeding Centre for Endangered Species. The center's mission of saving endangered species takes on a new resonance in light of the surprises of mortality the morning has dealt, and the sensation of a cheetah licking our hands, the sound of its buzz-saw purr, the amber flame in the big cat's eyes, are affirmations of life.

If lunch has a subdued note, the sheer beauty and luxuriance of the Lowveld militate against gloom. Wildebeest, zebra, and impala stare up at us as we trundle through game reserves on an elevated rail bed. Cape buffalo stand stock still at our apparition, snort, and stampede. I'm reminded of movies of the Old West, scenes of Eastern greenhorns gazing at endless herds of bison from carriages not so different from the ones we're riding.

Late in the day we climb again up mountain switchbacks. After the game country, we've been traveling through one of South Africa's more genteel and gentrified corners, broad valleys and tall hillsides of trimmed tea plantations, lush green orchards, and groomed commercial forests of planted pines. Now in the mountains, we leave European Africa for the older, indigenous one.

<hr/>

THE ONE AND ONLY COMPLAINT I'VE HEARD FROM SOME PASSENGERS IS THE LACK of contact with the cultures through which we're passing. It's one I can understand, especially for one-time visitors to South Africa who will see it only out their windows. But a luxury train, it seems to me, is not an ecotour, and Rovos Rail delivers what it promises. Yet I'm glad when we stop on a mountain trestle near a village at dusk, deep in the tribal heartland of the Venda, awaiting our dinnertime while the villagers prepare theirs. The mud-brick, reed-roofed round houses seem grown out of the mountainside's red earth, and the only electricity is on our train.

Dogs bark, a baby cries, children laugh, and women call in the mountain quiet. The train breathes, dusk settles, cooking fires wink on. The wood smoke comes to us, for me the smell of African campfires mingled with the sweet-acrid incense of a village still close to nature. It's the smell of a thousand dusks I've been lucky enough to know since I fell in love, first with this continent, then with its daughter Sigrid.

A bat appears, hunting in the cone of light behind the observation car's open platform. We watch in fascination as it dips and soars, zooming in and out of the darkness. The train starts up, and the bat follows. It flies with us a long way, past forests and high-banked cuts, under overhanging cliffs, round twists and turns, until the utter blackness of a tunnel swallows us up.

THROUGH THE WINDSCREEN OF THE SHINING SILVER BIRD, SPRAY FROM VICTORIA Falls comes into view like a pillar of smoke when our DC-4 is still 40 miles away. The craft's interior, though remodeled with up-to-date business-class airliner seats, still has a look and feel and an elusive, ineffable scent that recall my earliest airplane travels, in the 1950s with my expatriate family, when propellers were what made airplanes go, and air hostesses were called stewardesses and wore hats. When pilot Tony van Eeden invites me to the cockpit for the flight and landing, he speaks to the six-year-old who wore a Pan Am pilot's hat to bed for months after his first trans-Pacific passage.

The lobby of the Victoria Falls Hotel is the last stop on our itinerary, where Rovos Rail officially signs off as host. It's a worthy destination, a marble-and-mahogany palace in a league with the Mount Nelson. Opened in 1904, soon after the railroad reached the natural wonder of the falls, it helped make them an international must-see for the well traveled. Though Rhodes didn't live to see it, his railroad went on to link South Africa with British colonies from here to the Equator, if never to Cairo.

Today Victoria Falls is a magnet for thrill seekers, with bungee jumpers dangling off the rail bridge, now with a road as well, that soars over the Zambezi River Gorge, while adventurers of all ages raft down Class VI rapids hundreds of feet beneath it. But on the hotel's terrace at teatime, when scones with cream and strawberry jam arrive in three-tiered confectionary baskets, the pleasures are, well, Victorian.

In the still air of dawn the plume of spray towers a thousand or more feet above the terrace, intimidating as a looming giant. Still more overwhelming are the falls themselves, easily reached if you hike along the Zimbabwean shore a short way from the hotel, or walk over the dizzying bridge to see the main falls from Zambia. They're a curtain of plunging water a mile long, longest in the world, a collision of falling water and stone thunderous to shouting level, their spray blasting up the opposite cliffs in a hurricane that blots out the sun, then falls in a constant drizzle onto rain forests nurtured by the eternal deluge.

Away from the falls, the air is bright with rainbows in the fine mist that swirls overhead. Above the river's muted grumble we hear another sound, the familiar click-clack of wheels on trestles, the deep thrumming of carriages crossing the bridge, then the whistle of a train.

It might just as well be Rohan's trans-Africa special headed for Dar es Salaam, 1,988 miles out of Cape Town with 1,800 miles to go to the Indian Ocean. Maybe one time, I say to Sigrid, we'll be on it. She smiles, ready to sign up.

So is it a train, I wonder, or where it takes us, that gives us the urge for going? Or might they be one and the same?

THE SIERRA MADRE EXPRESS

By Scott Thybony

Photos by
Phil Schermeister

A clang of heavy metal brings me awake, eyes wide open, as the rumbling of the train shifts a notch in tempo.

Outside the window a new morning unrolls somewhere deep in Mexico. Just where, I'm not sure. One of the pleasures of a train journey is to fall asleep and wake up somewhere far away from where you started, to be transported.

Checking the map, I find we're crossing the coastal plains of Sinaloa straight toward the legendary Sierra Madre Occidental. This vast cordillera runs 700 miles down the spine of Mexico, and we're heading for its rugged core, a convergence of immense canyons known as the Copper Canyon country. Our train will climb from near sea level to more than 8,000 feet in elevation, traveling from a land of parrots and palm trees to a high country of evergreens and winter snowfall.

Warm and lucent, the morning light has a softer quality to it than yesterday's desert sun. Even the air has an unfamiliar scent as I step onto the platform between cars and lean into the wind the way a dog rides in the back of a pickup. A slight tang of salt comes from the Gulf of California to the west, mixing with wood smoke and the faint aroma of strange, flowering plants. Above a wide field spreads a wider sky, flanked by adobe homes painted a shade of pink matching the backyard flowers.

With a whoosh, the car door opens, and trainmaster Mike Cowan walks toward me, swaying from side to side with the jostle of the train. The crew shunted the engine from one end of the train to the other, switching onto the new line as the passengers slept. We're now ahead of schedule and all is well. "Good morning!" he says with a big grin.

The trainmaster runs the show for *Sierra Madre Express*, a private rail company conducting weeklong excursions from Tucson to Copper Canyon.

PRECEDING PAGES: *Giant saguaro cactuses reach skyward in Sonora. Vegetation changes dramatically along the route of travel, beginning in the desert, passing foothill villages growing mangoes and bananas, and ending high in the evergreen forests bordering Copper Canyon.*

For ten years, Mike has looked after the safety and comfort of his passengers, supervised a crew of seven cooks and porters, and coordinated schedules with the Mexican railroad. And that's just the start of his duties. He's now wearing a cowboy hat, but as responsibilities change he'll actually switch hats, putting on a cap with long earflaps when there's serious work ahead. A medical volunteer and a bilingual host also accompany the passengers on a journey that will cover more than 1,300 miles by rail.

As our train rounds a curve, the green-and-red FerroMex engine swings into view. It pulls a string of five restored railcars, painted gray with a pair of red stripes. They include a lounge car, an observation dome that also serves as the dining car, and Pullman sleepers. My stateroom has a foldaway upper bunk, a shallow closet, a toilet, and a fold-up sink. But I don't spend much time there, taking advantage of the freedom to move about. When you get restless, you can walk the length of the train, staggering down the aisles as you time your stride to the sway and lurch of the train.

Reaching the last car, I watch the rails spool out behind

SIERRA MADRE EXPRESS

us as the flags of Mexico and the United States flutter from the rear. Gus Gustafson and his son and daughter-in-law have settled into seats on the open-air deck of the Divisadero car. Gus was one of the first passengers on the maiden run of the *Sierra Madre Express* in 1981 and has returned to celebrate his birthday. Gus came to Arizona more than 50 years ago when a doctor gave him six months to live. "It's been a long six months," he says with a smile.

As it does on a river trip, a camaraderie soon develops among the passengers, spurred in part by the knowledge we will soon part ways. Charlie Hatfield, a railroad buff wearing a yellow Union Pacific cap, tells me he would be content to spend every night on the train. His fascination with railroading stems from his childhood in Kentucky. When he was six years old, his parents would put him on a train alone, where he loved to ride on the vestibule between the cars. "When my grandparents met me on the other end," he says, "I'd be covered in coal dust and soot."

On a train journey you become a true passenger again, not just a piece of cargo shuttled from one terminal to the next. You take in the changing views from each car and eat, talk with other passengers, and eat again. Then it's time for lunch. The food, carried from the States along with all water and ice, comes nonstop if you let it. Between scheduled meals, you find snacks close at hand wherever you take a seat, and if they happen to be beyond reach, just wait. At regular intervals, the porter brings around a snack tray when he's not serving drinks.

The tremendous scale of the landscape soon swallows the train as we leave the *tierra caliente*, the hot lowlands, and close in on the Sierra Madre. The mountain front rises ahead in a massive wall appearing unbroken from a distance. It fills the horizon from north to south, enclosing some of the

Mission bells hang silent outside San Xavier del Bac near Tucson,
Arizona. Centuries ago, Spanish priests built a network of missions
as they explored what is now the American Southwest and traveled
deep into the canyons of the Sierra Madre.

most rugged terrain in North America and an ecological borderland where mountain, desert, and subtropical zones crowd together.

Arms of cardón cactus spike through the thorn forest covering hills of hardened lava. A fuzzy yellow fruit, used by the local Indians as a hairbrush, hangs from the cactus, and everywhere bare branches intertwine to blanket the slopes. When the summer rains come they will leaf out in only a few days, and suddenly the hills will transform into a lush forest. Everything in the landscape has subtly changed since we boarded the train, or almost everything. The dogs remain the same wherever you travel in Mexico. A scrawny, mud-colored mutt stands stiff-legged in the middle of a dirt street, watching the train zip past.

Each mud-brick village along the way has its own character. One has a derelict appearance, as if the residents planned to stay only through a single planting. The next village down the line is solidly rooted with fruit trees shading each home, whitewashed walls, and streets so clean they appear to be hand-swept. These farming communities move with the slow rhythm of the seasons, jarred momentarily by the rush of the passing train.

At the next station, a young field hand sits in the back of a pickup strumming his guitar among the papaya and mango trees. Large corporate farms worked with heavy machinery lie behind us, and as the land becomes rockier the fields shrink. A lone farmer in a straw hat now walks behind a horse-drawn plow. When we reach the high country, Tarahumara Indians will be planting their plots with digging sticks much the way their ancestors did a thousand years ago. We may not be traveling back in time, but leaving behind centuries of technological change comes close.

Landing in the Arizona car, I find several passengers watching *The Treasure of the Sierra Madre* on a VCR. In the Hollywood classic, an old prospector played by Walter Huston is riding a train into the Sierra Madre during the 1920s. He stares at the map on his knees, searching for the most remote corner of Mexico. "We gotta go where there's no trails at all," he tells his young partner, "where you can be positive that no surveyor or anybody who knows anything about prospecting has ever been there before."

The Sierra remains remote country, but even in the 1920s it was not a blank spot on the map. Spanish missionaries and miners crisscrossed it centuries earlier, founding El Fuerte, a town we just passed, as a military outpost in 1564. But the mountains still have plenty of hard-to-reach corners, and a sense of remoteness takes hold as the train crosses the Río Fuerte. Checking the rail log, I find the bridge spans an incredible 1,637 feet, the longest on the line. Far below, a vaquero leads a string of horses across a ford. It being the dry season, the river is running low, exposing a boulder-choked streambed.

A porter masters the art of serving dessert on a swaying train as passengers watch sunset from the dining car. Timed to cross the desert at night, the Sierra Madre Express *begins its climb into the mountains at daybreak.*

OPPOSITE: *Tracks curve below jagged peaks as the train crosses the Río Mina Plata on what travel writers have voted "the world's most exciting train ride." Building a railroad across the rugged Sierra took 35 bridges and 87 tunnels.*

Trackside vendors at El Divisadero tempt visitors with local fare cooked over open grills. Passengers on the Sierra Madre Express *get their first expansive view of Copper Canyon as they leave the train here to spend two nights in a cliffside lodge.*

OPPOSITE: *Baskets and weavings crowd the station platform to catch the attention of arriving passengers. Tarahumara Indian women often sell their handicrafts at train stops. Now numbering some 70,000 people, most Tarahumara scratch out a living as small-scale farmers and herders.*

We are entering the Sierra Tarahumara, the highest and most isolated section of the Sierra Madre. Here the headwaters of the Río Fuerte carve a complex of immense canyons along the western edge of the state of Chihuahua. The most famous of these is la Barranca del Cobre, known as Copper Canyon. The name refers to both a single canyon and the region surrounding it. Before long, the train enters El Descanso, the first and longest tunnel on the line. After being submerged in darkness for more than two minutes, we rocket into the sunlight at the far end more than a mile away. In some sections of the line, the train threads through so many tunnels we log nearly as much dark time as daylight.

The train rounds a bend and trundles across a thousand-foot bridge, so narrow it disappears from sight. Trying to find where it went, I look down and see a horseman crossing a suspension bridge over the Río Chinipas, 350 feet below. The country keeps growing wilder, studded with broken crags and filled with strange plants. Octopus agave grow from the cliffs in hanging gardens, their limp leaves appearing more like tidal life-forms than mountain growth. Blood red branches of the madrone twist upward, and wild figs cling to the cliff rock. "I love the way those fig roots melt down the rock," says botanist Meg Quinn.

At Témoris, founded by Jesuit missionaries in the 17th century, three levels of track can be seen. Our train crosses the Río Septentrión on a curving trestle and slowly comes to a stop, nose to nose with a freight train. It appears to be a Mexican standoff until we yield the right-of-way and back onto a siding. The descending locomotive pulls tank cars filled with corn sweeteners and flatcars carrying logs. When we leave the siding, a crewman jumps down and throws the switch by hand. Trains crossing the Sierra run without electric signals or computers, keeping to their schedules with the aid of timetables, watches, and radios—the way it used to be done everywhere.

Immediately ahead, the tracks disappear into the famous La Pera tunnel. The train enters the mountain and makes a 180-degree turn while covering 3,074 feet underground. It emerges into daylight on the same mountainside but headed in the opposite direction. Those sitting on the left side of the cars look down the canyon on the way in and those on the right get their chance when it exits. In areas prone to landslides, arches have been built to shelter the rail bed from falling rock. As we gain elevation, thickets of manzanita and Chihuahua oak grade into ponderosa and Durango pines.

Steadily climbing, the *Sierra Madre Express* winds through a canyon in cliff-hugging curves. On one side a rock face juts out as angular as a jawbone, and on the opposite slope steep talus falls into the gorge. The river below cascades into plunge pools and braids among the boulders. Everywhere the land appears upturned or downcut, a dynamic landscape where raw geological forces are still at work. On this stretch of track, the train passes through 16 tunnels in only 12 miles. Sometimes the tail of the train hasn't left the last tunnel before the engine enters the next.

The railway began as a visionary scheme in the 19th century to shorten the shipping distance between Kansas City and the Pacific by 400 miles. Construction started in 1885, but revolution, bankruptcy, and the incredibly rugged terrain forced abandonment of the project more than once. Only after marshaling thousands of workers and considerable engineering skill did the Mexican government complete the rail system in 1961. Tracks now cross the Sierra Madre, running for more than 400 miles from Los Mochis to Chihuahua with the aid of 35 major bridges and 87 tunnels. The government privatized the railroad in 1998, and a few months later, in a scene straight from the Wild West, banditos commandeered the FerroMex train. They forced it to halt in a tunnel and robbed the passengers at gunpoint.

By mid-afternoon we arrive at El Divisadero and run a gantlet of vendors to reach the Copper Canyon overlook. Here Tarahumara women sell baskets woven from sotol leaves and the long-needled Apache pine. The Indian women dress traditionally in brightly colored skirts and full blouses, and cover their heads with scarves. The men wear jeans and cowboy hats, but in more remote areas some still prefer a loose-fitting cotton shirt and a loincloth. Both wear thong sandals made from discarded tires.

A few feet in front of us the rimrock falls away into empty space where two tributary canyons intersect the main branch carved by the Río Urique. The Spanish word *barranca*, referring to terrain that breaks away sharply into steeply eroded slopes, works better than canyon. With more talus than cliff and more brush than bare rock, Copper Canyon gives the impression of two mountain ranges facing each other rather than a sheer-walled gorge. The temptation to compare it with the Grand Canyon is misleading; each has its own unique beauty. Years ago I came here, riding the second-class train with a crew of drunken lumbermen and a potbellied stove in the corner. To return to the barrancas is like meeting an old friend.

Thin shadows edge the ravines below, but the depth of field is lost in the flat haze of midday. With two nights set aside in a cliffside lodge, we'll

FOLLOWING PAGES: *The world falls away where Copper Canyon, la Barranca del Cobre, breaks through the crest of the Sierra Madre. Guests at the Posada Mirador can watch sunset from private balconies overlooking the deeply eroded landscape.*

have time to encounter the canyon in all its moods. A bus takes us a couple of miles to the Posada Mirador, a hotel built on the very rim. Each room is decorated with custom-made furniture and has a private balcony overlooking the barranca. On her first visit, tour host Ann Brehm-Moline was surprised to find such a fine hotel in the middle of nowhere. "The plumbing is marvelous," she says. "They *have* plumbing—that's what's marvelous."

That night Tarahumara families join us to watch one of their men perform traditional dances accompanied by local musicians. He does a deer dance, followed by a donkey dance and a bull dance with no discernible variation in the songs and steps. Wrapped around his legs are strings of rattles made from the cocoons of saturniid moths. To make them, the Indians insert a pebble inside each cocoon before sewing it to the string. After the show, the performers and their families trail back to their homes in the canyon.

＝>◆<＝

AT DAWN A FAINT LIGHT DRAWS THE HIGHEST CLIFFS FROM THE DARKNESS. THE gorge appears bottomless. Ridges and peaks emerge from a blue-gray haze of smoke and distance. The canyon slope drops steeply below the rim, covered by a mantle of broken rock and brush. Somewhere below a dog barks, sharp and clear, and waits as if listening for its own echo before barking again. Soon a rooster crows from a rancho on a distant ridge top, answered by another nearby. Many of the Indian farmsteads blend in so well you are aware of their presence only by seeing campfires at night or hearing their roosters.

Hummingbirds are already stirring on the terrace, zinging up to the feeders and back to the trees, when Fred Masciangelo from Maine joins me. We engage in the morning ritual of gazing into the canyon with a cup of coffee in hand. "If we ever have a major catastrophe," he says, "these Tarahumara, who already live on nothing, are the only ones who will survive."

Before breakfast, I follow a trail below to a cliff house within sight of the lodge. Many Tarahumara live in rock shelters without electricity or running water. This house, more substantial than most, is made of adobe brick and roofed with wooden shakes. Thin shavings of meat hang in the open air to dry, making jerky for later storage. A mother takes a siesta in the shade of the overhang, while an older daughter brings in the laundry. The Tarahumara lived here long before the lodge came and have found no reason to leave.

When I walk to an overlook, a young Tarahumara boy appears and offers me a handful of quartz crystals for sale. He doesn't speak Spanish, and when I show no interest in buying he climbs a nearby rock. Standing in his sandals on the brink of a sheer, 50-foot drop, he waits until he has my attention and jumps. I know he's up to something, but there's a moment of uncertainty until he climbs up smiling from a hidden ledge.

That morning we reboard the train and head for the lumber town of

Creel, 30 miles up the line. Along the way, outcrops of volcanic tuff have weathered into a natural masonry of piled stone and broken columns. At El Lazo the tracks twist into a loose knot, one of the few places in the world where they loop over themselves. In these barrancas, the shortest distance between two points happens to be a route that curves and bends back upon itself as wildly as a pretzel. We soon top the Continental Divide; at 8,071 feet it's the highest point on the line.

Creel has come into its own with a string of streetlights and recently paved roads, but a couple of horses wandering down the street help it retain its frontier atmosphere. After a quick look around, Tarahumara guide Pedro Palma takes us on a 12-mile bus ride to the traditional village of Cusárare, the "Place of the Eagles." To avoid disrupting the lives of the

Spanish and Indian traditions influence the region's decorative art. A wall niche displays ollas made by Tarahumara potters for cooking and carrying water. At every turn, visitors find items crafted by a people who still make much of what they need.

Tarahumara women, dressed in bright skirts and head scarves,
offer baskets for sale to passengers on the observation deck.
The Indians often walk long miles to meet the scheduled trains
and then return to their canyon homes in the evening.

OPPOSITE: A basketmaker prepares leaves of the desert sotol, which
she has gathered to weave into large baskets in a variety of patterns.
She also uses the long needles of the Apache pine for the smaller
baskets sold to tourists.

FOLLOWING PAGES: A passenger detrains at the village of Bahuichivo
as a burro waits patiently for the packer to load supplies. In a land
where roads are few, the burro remains a standard means of
transporting goods from the railway to remote homesteads.

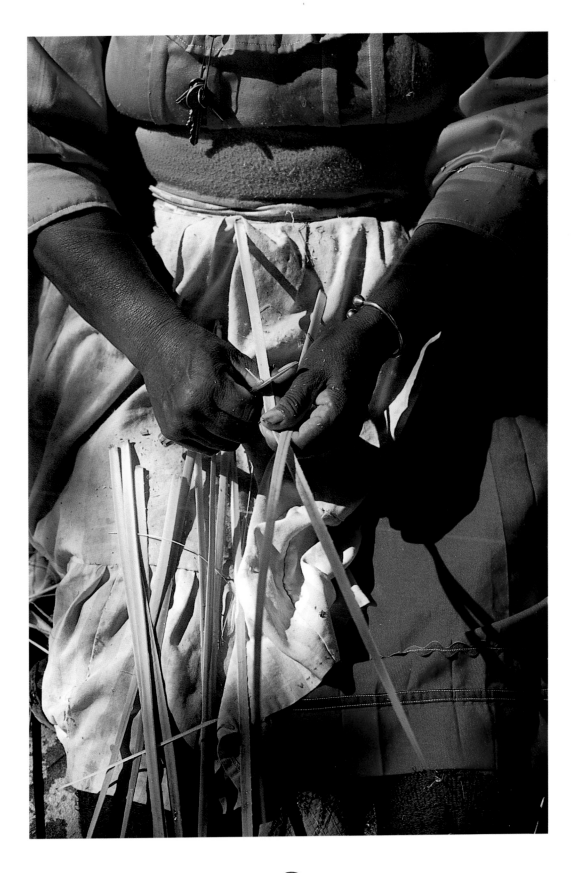

local people, Pedro stops only at the cave home of Doña Petra on the outskirts of Creel. She lives in a rock shelter with nine of her children and grandchildren. Soot covers the low ceiling inside, creating a permanent night sky. To keep people from bumping their heads, she has rubbed off the black on the lowest projections to expose the lighter rock underneath. Those taking photos leave some dollars behind as a courtesy.

"We probably made her day," says passenger Folger Gifford as we depart.

"The money we left here," Pedro says, "is what she would make in three days of cutting firewood, packing it on a donkey, and carrying it to town to sell. You didn't make her day, you made her week."

AN ESTIMATED 70,000 TARAHUMARA INDIANS INHABIT THE CANYON COUNTRY of the Sierra Madre. They never hit their children, expressing this gentleness in their handshake, a slight brushing of the fingers. They place greater value on personal relations than business, have no swear words in their native language, and share whatever food they have. Corn beer, *tesguino*, plays a major role in their social gatherings and is often given as compensation for help in the fields or building a house. Typically, a Tarahumara will spend a hundred days a year brewing and drinking tesguino— and recovering from it.

Drug traffickers have made inroads into the lives of the Tarahumara, sometimes coercing villagers to aid them. Since the Indians already live in the most remote canyons, having fled from Spanish rule three centuries ago, they have nowhere left to run. But other Tarahumara have freely chosen to grow marijuana. "When you have nothing," says Pedro, "the temptation is high."

Each Sunday in Cusárare, the village leaders meet with the local men in the courtyard to conduct community affairs. The women, dressed in their Sunday best and carrying babies in shawls, wait for their men to finish so the church services can begin. Jesuits founded the mission of Nuestra Señora de Guadalupe here about 1744 and restored the church in the 1970s after years of neglect. It is one of the finest Spanish colonial churches in the Sierra Tarahumara.

We pass through its thick adobe walls into the cool interior. There are no pews, so the faithful kneel to pray on the hand-hewn floorboards. They have decorated the walls of the sanctuary with traditional designs taken from their woven sashes. Above the altar hangs a painting of the Virgin of Guadalupe, and in a side chapel some villagers have burned incense before a human skull. When the flooring was replaced, they found the skull of a young man buried beneath the church and decided to place it near the altar.

Pedro leads Antonio Camilo, a Tarahumara musician, to the front and asks him to play the *chapareke*, a traditional string instrument. Pedro introduces him as the last master of the chapareke and says he walked several hours from his home this morning to attend church. The musician stands holding the end of a hollow agave stalk next to his mouth and strums the three strings, playing the instrument much like a jaw harp. He finishes a lively folk tune and shyly smiles when we applaud.

A smoke haze hangs in the distance, visible on the ride back to Creel. Pedro tells me the fires are set purposely during the dry season to bring rain. "The Tarahumara," he says, "believe smoke will bring clouds, so they start fires to bring rain. The government tries to stop them, but they keep doing it."

When we first stepped off the train at Creel, we had been warned not to give the kids any money or candy to keep them from swarming the platform. But donations are encouraged through local organizations that know what is needed and how to minimize the impact on the local culture. Over the years, the train crew has found ways to make a difference in the lives of their Tarahumara friends, routinely bringing school and medical supplies across the border. Mike, the trainmaster, tells me they have delivered a respirator and an x-ray machine to the hospital, solar panels for a boarding school, and even treadle sewing machines.

He leads me and Jo Sullivan-Hayes, an emergency room nurse, past the mission craft shop to the children's hospital, Clinica Santa Teresita. Built in 1965, it has 75 beds and a staff of 5 doctors and 7 nurses, plus about 20 student nurses and assistants. Jo checks out the emergency room while Mike talks with friends. Everything is so antique," she says, "but incredibly clean. For what they have, they do an awesome job." She notices the mended sheets and disposable gloves washed for reuse. "When I see this, it makes me mad. We throw away so much."

Local Indians suffer from malnutrition and intestinal diseases, especially in dry years. The Catholic mission reports 3,000 children may have died last year when the worst drought in ten years destroyed the corn and bean crops. Father Luis Verplancken, a Jesuit priest who has spent his life

FOLLOWING PAGES: *Men gather after work to talk on the cobblestone streets of Batopilas. Lying on the floor of a deep canyon, the Spanish colonial town served as the center of an important silver-mining district for nearly two centuries.*

*Students chat between classes at the Tarahumara boarding school
in the village of Cerocahui. Two girls wear traditional thong
sandals, and many come from distant homes without electricity
or running water.*

An image of the Virgin of Guadalupe greets the faithful inside the church at Cerocahui. Father Andres Lara began rebuilding the ruined church during the 1940s and established the boarding school.

among the Tarahumara, estimates that 40 percent of the children will die before the age of five. To prevent starvation and illness, the mission distributes food in remote villages and drills wells to provide safe drinking water.

That evening at the lodge, Andy Anderson, a pecan grower from Texas, carves up his chicken dinner. "Do you reckon," he wonders, "this is the rooster that woke me up this morning?"

NEXT MORNING I JOIN BARBARA KNUDSON FROM VERMONT ON A HIKE INTO THE canyon. The air smells of dry grass and sun-warmed pine needles. A mother and her daughters approach us, walking barefoot up the trail. She's one of the basket weavers who work outside the lodge. When we pass she covers her mouth with a corner of her shawl and then looks back with a smile. We continue descending for a couple of miles and stop at the Tarahumara rancho of Wakajípare.

The homestead lies between spur ridges where the canyon funnels into a narrows. It consists of a cabin, a goat pen, a chicken coop raised on stilts, and a well-built storehouse for staple foods such as corn and beans, squash, and maybe some apples and a few chilies. Behind the dwelling they've planted a cornfield on a slope so steep you'd roll down it if you slipped. Goat trails crisscross the grassy slopes below. With such a high infant-mortality rate and low life expectancy, their way of life is difficult. I've seen the water they drink and the dark, smoky interior of their homes. But the idea of living simply, of spending your days in a cabin perched high on a canyonside, still has a pull to it.

When we take a water break on the hike back, I notice an old Tarahumara man coming up the back of the ridge. He sees us and instinctively slips behind a scrub oak, turns sideways, and to my surprise he disappears. How anyone can hide behind such a skinny tree is a mystery, but seeing no threat he quickly steps out. When we start up the trail again, I motion to him and pretend I want to race. He's half my size but would instantly leave me in the dust. Thankfully, he just laughs.

I once saw a Tarahumara running down a trail with such grace I mistook him for a deer. Known for their tremendous endurance, Tarahumara run footraces covering up to a hundred miles across rocky mountainsides while tossing a wooden ball with their feet. Runners from the Sierra have competed in races outside their homeland, doing well when they are allowed to compete in tire sandals and eat pinole, a trail food made from ground corn. In 1994, Tarahumara Juan Herrara set the course record on the grueling Leadville Trail hundred-mile race, reaching elevations up to

12,620 feet in the Colorado Rockies. But back home the goal isn't to set records. The staggering bets placed on the races give the runners a motive to push their hardest. "Sometimes," said Pedro Palma, "the winner is whoever is left standing."

Our party reboards the train and by evening has settled into a new lodge at Cerocahui. In this remote village roses bloom next to doorways and plowed fields roll out to the foot of the surrounding mountains. A Jesuit mission was founded in 1680. Today, the town of 900 inhabitants is dominated by a red-stone church dating to 1741 and reconstructed in 1948. A burro hauls a load of firewood down a street as sunbaked as the adobe homes crowding the plaza. A couple of general stores are tucked in among them almost as an afterthought. Business is not the preoccupation of these people. Masons, working on a wall in the plaza, shape the stone with hand-forged axes; the handles have been cut and shaved by hand. They volunteer their labor, putting in an hour or two before returning home to other chores.

A vineyard on the grounds of the Hotel Misión, a former hacienda, produces table wines served at dinner. Rising above the grapevines is a giant nopal, a spineless cactus as tall as a tree. Rooms, set around a landscaped courtyard, have kerosene lamps and wood-burning stoves for heat. Next to the hotel lies a Catholic boarding school for Tarahumara girls, serving 70 residents and more than 200 day students during a school year lasting from September to June. The nuns say the students dread going home at the end of the term because they will have nothing to eat. They have been collecting as much food as possible to send with them, and many train passengers generously help the effort when they learn of the need.

Power lines are heading toward Cerocahui, so much will change. But for now, a boy rides by on horseback, and across the river men plant their fields by hand. Pigeons coo and a goat bleats from a backyard; wood smoke drifts on the air. At long intervals, a truck rumbles along the main road, leaving the village even quieter with its passing. Nothing stirs at night as a stillness settles in, a single moment suspended between dusk and dawn. Morning brings with it the sounds of another era. Roosters call back and forth, horses neigh, and birds rustle in the branches overhead and begin to chitter. Then the hotel generator kicks in and the lights come on.

Later we take a retired school bus, the main form of mass transit here,

FOLLOWING PAGES: *Storm clouds build over the western slope of the 700-mile-long Sierra Madre range. At its foot, farmers use the stored waters of the Río Fuerte, whose upper branches have carved the region's deepest canyons, to irrigate their fields.*

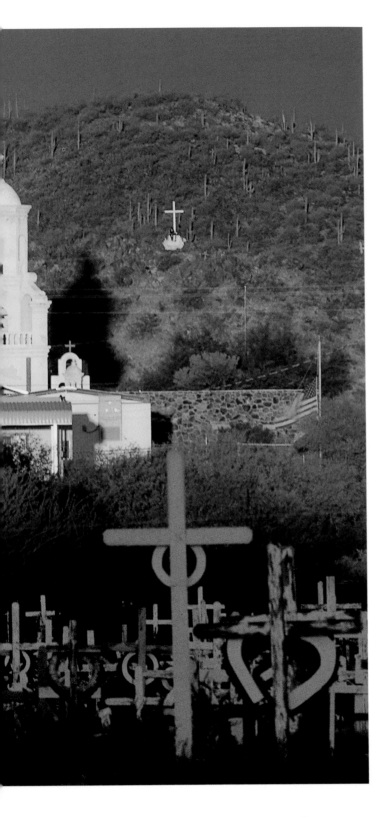

Wooden crosses fill a cemetery next to San Xavier del Bac. Known as the White Dove of the Desert, the mission church catches the last glow of sunset. Father Eusebio Kino founded a string of 24 missions, including San Xavier, between 1687 and 1711.

to Cerro del Gallego. This viewpoint overlooks the lower end of Copper Canyon and the old mining town of Urique. For nearly two centuries, the barrancas were one of the most important silver-mining regions in northern Mexico with veins of ore so massive miners had to hack them out with axes. The road leaves the valley and climbs into the mountains above. On the ridge top, a wooden cross marks a place of resting and prayer for the Tarahumara who make long pilgrimages to Cerocahui during Holy Week.

The road threads between patches of shade and sunlight, between old burns and thickets of bracken fern and Tarahumara oak. A man and his wife use digging sticks to plant a field below the road, moving slowly in a day-long rhythm. Not far beyond, we stop at La Virgencita, a roadside shrine where travelers have burned candles and left green cuttings as offerings. Water seeps from the ceiling of the alcove, and I open my mouth to catch a few drips—the right impulse, it turns out. Among the locals, the spring is thought to be a fountain of youth.

A bend or two farther brings us to the overlook. Urique lies in the deepest reaches of the canyon more than a mile below us, where a twist of river flashes as bright as chrome. Across the gorge, ridges stack up one behind the next, fading into each other and finally into the distance. The narrow road continues into the canyon, snaking downward in dozens of tight switchbacks, but our party turns back at this point. We have a train to catch.

The *Sierra Madre Express* has timed its departure from the mountains to cross the most spectacular stretch of tracks during the daylight hours. Back at the station, we board the train for the last time and retrace our inbound route. As we leave the Sierra, evening light falls across the western slopes, painting the rock with a soft incandescence. The last reds soon drain from all but the highest ridges, and each tree throws a long shadow lasting until the sky switches abruptly to night.

In the dark I settle into the familiar swaying rhythm of the train and let my thoughts catch up. By returning to the Copper Canyon country after many years, I found it has changed in obvious ways, but the changes have not transformed its unique character. The great canyons have not lost their capacity to renew a sense of wonder, to carry you away. The heart of the Sierra, sometimes elusive and always intriguing, remains intact.

A passenger finds a perch on the canyon's edge for a final view of Mexico's high country before catching the departing train. The Sierra Madre Express crosses its highest point at the Continental Divide, 8,071 feet in elevation. Many Tarahumara leave the mountains during winter and descend into the warmer canyons.

The Royal Scotsman

By Ron Fisher

Photos by
Tino Soriano

To the melancholy skirling of a kilted piper, we march along the train's platform,

like schoolchildren on a day trip. We would make an unusual class: We are mostly middle-aged or above, for one thing, and most of the men are in jackets or blazers and the women in smart traveling outfits. There are no T-shirts or shorts. The men are tan and fit. Probably golfers. The women look confident and expectant.

The piper is magnificent—a large man, with red cheeks, impeccably got up in kilt and bonnet and full piper regalia. He's playing "The Heights of Cassino." People at the station stand and stare as we march by. Little children point.

We board our train and are directed to an observation car at its tail end, where we dispose ourselves on various comfortable sofas and armchairs. The staff, nodding and smiling, all seem to know our names already. "Good afternoon, Mr. Fisher," they say. "Welcome aboard."

We have just boarded the *Royal Scotsman*, which bills itself as "the world's most exclusive train." It carries just 36 passengers when full—no children under 12—on trips of one, two, or four days throughout Scotland. Price for the four-day trip, per person, is a stately $4,350—a little over a thousand dollars a day. Per person. If you had looked closely at that group marching along the platform, you might have noticed that most of us appear to have, on the whole, more money than is quite good for us.

The train, according to its literature, offers "a revival of the romantic age of railway travel, combining Edwardian splendor with modern luxury." Owned and operated by the Great Scottish and Western Railway Company, it consists of nine cars: two dining cars, the open-ended observation car, a

PRECEDING PAGES: *Sheep dot a peaceful hillside near Dunkeld. Such bucolic scenes are common from the windows of the* Royal Scotsman, *which devotes leisurely days and nights to a luxurious tour of the Highlands of Scotland.*

service car for the crew, and five cars composed of either single or double cabins. Most of the cars were ordinary Pullmans transformed by a shop-fitting company in Bournemouth into the elegant carriages they are today. They've been operating, in their present configuration as the *Royal Scotsman*, since 1990—time enough to have earned a worldwide reputation for

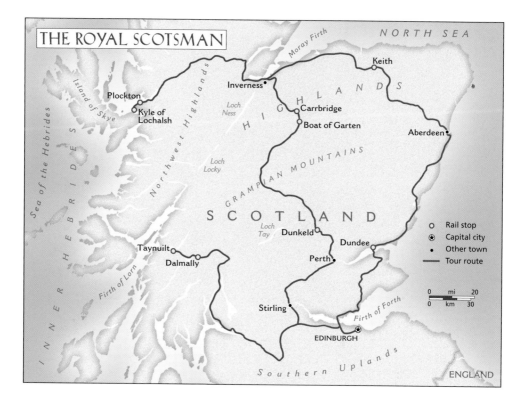

THE ROYAL SCOTSMAN

service, relaxed elegance, and fine dining. I feel a little like the beggar at the feast as we lounge in the observation car, sipping champagne, clearly out of my league. We meet our tour guide, Marilyn Hunter. Marilyn will be our companion for the next four days, making certain we're comfortable and happy, and accompanying us on various day trips by bus. Our tour will take us through the spectacular southern Highlands, with its glens, lochs, and waterfalls, into the grandeur of the northwestern Highlands and the Isle of Skye; and finally through the rolling farmlands of the northeast.

I chat with Al and Susan from Tulsa as the train, with a gentle thump, gets under way. Al was "in food"—he oversaw several Little Caesar franchises—but sold everything and now is retired. "Every year my sister gives us a trip as a present," says Susan. "This year she overheard a woman in the supermarket talking about the *Royal Scotsman*, so this is our present for this year."

Nearby are Pat and her granddaughter Rachel. Rachel has the look of a mature college student, and we're all astonished to learn she's 13 years old and still has braces on her teeth. Pat, after a series of botched knee operations, is in a wheelchair; Rachel is here as companion and to push her along. Pat writes and lectures on gardening in California and appears to have one of those strong, forceful personalities that can get on people's nerves. We'll see.

As we roll through the outskirts of Edinburgh, one of the staff named Katie approaches. "Excuse me, Mr. Fisher," she says. "Would it be convenient for you to come now to see your cabin?"

Of course.

It's small but comfortable—55 square feet with a 15-square-foot bathroom that includes a shower. There's a bed and a ceiling fan and a tiny closet and a desk with a potted plant on it that looks like a kind of heather. The walls are rich marquetry, and heavy drapes hang at the window. There's a call button in case I feel like summoning a midnight snack. My luggage has mysteriously arrived before me and is waiting on the bed.

Left alone I unpack—everything fits, barely—and pause to peer out my window with that cozy feeling travelers get when they know they're

Piper Davie Hutton welcomes visitors to Gleneagles. The Romans evidently introduced bagpipes to Scotland, where they have been the distinctive voice of the country for centuries. Every autumn the World Piping Championships hosts world-class pipers.

settled into a comfortable place and don't have to move for a while. Outside, rural Scotland is whizzing past. In a letter Henry James wrote, "Once you get the hang of it, and apprehend the type, it is a most beautiful and admirable little country...." We're heading west from Edinburgh. We'll pass through Falkirk, skirt Glasgow, pass Clydebank and Dumbarton, then touch the northern bank of the Clyde. In the gray, drizzly afternoon, villages themselves are mostly gray; only the bright colors of automobiles relieve the somber tone. There's a flock of sheep on a hillside, so posed they look fake, like those pink flamingos people stick in their lawns.

I have a wash and go to the observation car for tea: scones and fruitcake, heavy cream and jams. The carriage's corridor is just two feet wide, so if you squeeze past someone, it's a fairly close encounter. In the observation car, the passengers are eyeing one another, being carefully polite, getting to know each other. There's a contingent of Germans, nine of them, with their own tour leader who has made the trip ten times. They keep to themselves.

In addition, there are two from Bermuda—"the Captain" and his jolly wife—two from the United Kingdom, two from the Netherlands, and fifteen from the United States. I talk with Don and Phoebe, from Charleston, South Carolina. They live on a barrier island off the coast and lost 31 trees in their backyard during Hurricane Hugo in 1989. Don says, "Everybody has to believe something, and I believe I'll have another scone."

One of the American passengers looks like a U.S. senator. His wife already seems bored, scowling at the horizon.

We pass another flock of sheep on a hillside, and three people say, simultaneously, "Sheep!" I stand for a while on the open platform at the rear of the car, where it's noisy but cool and fresh. Forests, streams, and lochs—or lakes—flash through the mist. The train, unlike many today that roll along smoothly quiet, makes a satisfying *clickety-clack.* There's a wind making the trees and bushes sway. A mighty waterfall tumbles down a bare mountain. The countryside looks wild and empty.

After Glasgow, we have Loch Lomond on our right and the Clyde on our left. The famous song about Loch Lomond was written by a soldier, dying far from home. He laments that while he will reach home before his companions, they will travel on the high road of life while he will be taking the low road, or death. Loch Lomond is the largest body of fresh water in Scotland, 24 miles long and .75 mile to 5 miles wide. Ancient stone walls, hoary with age, disappear into the underbrush.

At about 6 p.m., we arrive at Dalmally and disembark for a field trip. This train trip, in addition to being a pleasant ride, is meant to introduce us to Scottish history and culture, so we'll stop a couple of times a day for a visit to something either historic or cultural. At every stop we'll be met by

Ancient and impregnable, Edinburgh Castle looms over the heart of
the city. Its namesake king, Edwin, rebuilt an earlier fort here in the
6th century; between the 12th and 20th centuries the site was
treasury, royal palace, military garrison, and state prison.

OPPOSITE: *Nighttime traffic colors Princes Street beneath the towering
clock of Waverley Station, starting point for the* Royal Scotsman.
*Between late April and October, the train departs on one-, two-, and
four-day trips. The Scott Monument rises just beyond the station.*

FOLLOWING PAGES: *The ruins of Kilchurn Castle float in the mists of
Loch Awe. Over the centuries, castles were built all over the Scottish
Highlands as fortresses for warring clans. Kilchurn was abandoned in
the 18th century after being struck by lightning.*

a large bus, painted with the same colors and logo as the train, and its uni-formed driver, Alex. This is our first stop: the Inverawe Smokehouse.

Here Scottish salmon and trout are famously smoked. We troop off the bus and into the drizzle, where Alex hands each of us a huge *Royal Scotsman* umbrella for the ten-yard walk to the smokehouse. Owner Robert Camp-bell-Preston welcomes us to a chilly room that smells unmistakably of fish. Because of health regulations, we're each required to don a white smock and elasticized plastic cap. The senator's wife eyes her cap suspiciously. "Have these been worn by other people?" she asks. She stands by the door, capless, arms folded, glaring at the rain. Robert says, "A smoked fish is only as good as the one you start with." He demonstrates cold and hot smoking techniques and turns a herring into a kipper. He takes a smoked salmon and carefully slices it, the way you see it shrink-wrapped in the stores.

Escaping the drizzle, we go into his home where his wife, Rosie, has prepared a table of samples of all the products they market: salmon, trout, venison, fish patés, roast smoked salmon. We sample them all while sipping cool glasses of Pouilly-Fumé. Rosie says, "The tourist season got off to a slow start—the hoof-and-mouth business kept a lot of people away—but things have picked up in August." In the parlor, Rachel sits at a grand piano and bangs out a few bars of Scott Joplin's "The Entertainer."

On the bus ride back to the train, Pat lectures one couple on what was wrong with the Pouilly-Fumé and another on the proper pronunciation of *cómo está*. Pat may be a handful.

The train is "stabled" at Taynuilt Station, and when we arrive there one of the waiters, Alan, and the train manager, Camilla, are standing alongside it with trays of tall glasses of champagne. This is a feature that will repeat itself whenever we return to the train from one of our trips, and is always welcome.

We'll spend the night here at Taynuilt, for, as our tour literature says, "The *Royal Scotsman* stops each evening in a quiet siding or station to ensure you can enjoy a good night's rest."

Dinner aboard the train is fine: white bean and truffle soup, chicken with dauphinoise potatoes, chocolate tart. Even the waiters know every-one's name. I sit with Don and Phoebe, the Charleston couple. Don is 71 but looks 50. He has had severe heart problems in the past, so takes good care of himself. Years ago he was hired at IBM by Phoebe, whom he then mar-ried. Later he bought and sold private colleges. He's been retired 20 years. He plays the string bass in jazz bands, and also the tuba. He and Phoebe are great company, and the wine flows.

After dinner we all move to the observation car where a local accor-dionist named Paddy Shaw entertains. He, too, looks elegant in traditional kilt. As we sip our brandy, he plays mostly traditional Scottish songs, along with some *oom-pah* tunes for the Germans and, "for the Americans..." "Sweet Georgia Brown" and "Alexander's Ragtime Band."

"I'll finish with a wee elegant jig and some Burns songs, then 'Auld Lang Syne,' " he says.

Outside, the night has cleared and the Big Dipper hovers overhead. Cool Scottish breezes waft in the open window of my cabin, and I sleep, as they say, like a baby rock.

⟨⬦⟩

THIS DAY WILL REPEAT ITSELF, WITH VARIATIONS: TRAIN TRAVEL THROUGH THE magnificent scenery punctuated by excursions, meals, conversation, and sleep. People get to know one another and sort themselves into groups, though the Germans cluster together in the middle of our trip like an undigested sausage. They have brought their golf clubs and two or three times, instead of joining us on our field trips, they go off to play golf.

Our second morning we partly retrace yesterday's route, touching the shore of the River Clyde near Helensburgh. In his *Life of Scott*, J. G. Lockhart wrote, in 1838, "A voyage down the Clyde is enough to make anybody happy: nowhere can the home tourist, at all events, behold, in the course of one day, such a succession and variety of beautiful, romantic, and majestic scenery." We get off the train in Dunkeld, and there waiting with the bus is Alex. We pass through Birnam Wood, and Marilyn reads to us, over the perfectly tuned PA system in the bus, from *Macbeth*: "As I did stand my watch upon the Hill / I look'd toward Birnam, and anon, me thought / The Wood began to move...."

Dunkeld is an ancient village nearly destroyed in a Jacobite battle in 1689. The ruins of its cathedral, built between 1260 and 1501, stand beside the River Tay. Its north wall contains a leper's squint—a small hole through which lepers could see the altar during mass. Near Dunkeld, while on holiday in the countryside, Beatrix Potter found the inspiration for her Peter Rabbit stories.

Our destination this morning is the House of Bruar, which calls itself "Scotland's most prestigious country store." We're going shopping. The store's selection of cashmere items is especially fine, though there are clothing, china, glass, and gifts as well.

At least two of our number are eager for some shopping. Rachel, typical American teenager, could spend her life here. And Al, the former Little Caesar manager, is frantic. Because his sister-in-law arranged the trip, she was mailed all the literature by the train, which she neglected to share with Al. He thus had no way of knowing that two of the dinners aboard the train

Passengers aboard the Royal Scotsman *tour the Inverawe Smokehouse 80 miles north of Glasgow. Here local trout and salmon are cured and packaged for sale and export. Visitors comply with health regulations by wearing smocks and caps.*

Stabled at Taynuilt, the Royal Scotsman *resounds with the tunes of*
local accordionist Paddy Shaw, here performing in the observation
car after dinner. The train carries just 36 passengers when fully
booked—and no children under 12.

*Luncheon is served alfresco by waiter James Sankey at the rear of
the observation car as the farms and lochs of Scotland whiz past.
Storied home to kings and clansmen, the Highlands owe part of their
romantic appeal to the novels of Sir Walter Scott.*

OPPOSITE: *Wise beyond his years in the ways of fine cuisine, head chef
Nick Capon puts the finishing touches on a chicken and langoustine
salad. The train boasts one of the best restaurants in Britain—
moving or stationary. In 1998 Nick was a gold medalist in the finals
of Britain's National Chef of the Year competition.*

are meant to be formal, with the men in black tie. He has arrived in Scotland without so much as a sport coat so is ransacking the House of Bruar for a dark jacket that can pass for a tuxedo.

After lunch on the train—pan-roasted cod with crushed new potatoes, sticky toffee pudding with clotted cream—we once again board our bus. En route this time Marilyn tells us about the Scottish flag, an elegantly simple banner: a low-slung white cross on a rich blue background. It dates back at least to the 13th century, making it one of the oldest national flags in the world. The cross is also called the Cross of St. Andrew, supposedly because the saint was put to death by the Romans in Greece by being pinned to a cross of this shape.

There has been a powerful nationalist movement in Scotland in recent years, with many Scots agitating for independence from Great Britain. In 1997 they won a partial victory when they were given authority to elect a Scottish parliament in 1999, the first since 1707. It's a source of pride to many and scorn to some. The first year the parliament met, members got in trouble by devoting most of their time to working out salaries, bonuses, parking spaces, and vacation time for themselves. Scottish comic actor Billy Connolly dismissed them as "a wee pretendy parliament." Still, the 129-member body has the power to raise or lower income tax rates and settle local issues, while foreign relations, defense, and security will still be London's responsibility. And the new parliament has taken most of the steam out of the movement for total independence. As George Bernard Shaw wrote, "God help England if she had no Scots to think for her."

Scotland has castles the way Iowa has cornfields, and we visited two of them. At Ballindalloch Castle in the Spey Valley, on a morning turned sunny and bright, the Laird of Ballindalloch, Clare Nancy Macpherson-Grant, greets us on the lawn. Parts of the castle date from the early 16th century, and it has been in the laird's family since then, one of very few privately held castles to be lived in continuously by its original family. The laird oozes upper-class British charm as she welcomes us and tells us about the castle. "We know the first laird, Patrick Grant, acquired the land for the castle in 1532. The 12th laird, General James Grant, became governor of Florida in 1763 and fought in the American War of Independence. He was quite the epicurean and added the North Wing just to house his French chef.

"In 1860, the Third Baronet Sir George Macpherson-Grant founded the famous herd of Ballindalloch Aberdeen-Angus cattle, now the oldest herd in the world." They gaze at us with studied calm from a distance.

The laird notes that she has an unmarried son, the future laird, "so if any of you has an eligible daughter...." She manages to casually drop a famous name: "I was fortunate enough to have tea with the Queen Mother a few days ago...."

Upkeep of the castle is never ending and brutally expensive, which is why visitors and their entrance fees are welcomed. We stroll at leisure through the castle's beautiful rooms for an hour, then rest over a cup of tea.

We're stabled tonight at Boat of Garten on the Spey River. We're in the heart of the Scottish Highlands.

Scotland actually is a small country, a little smaller than South Carolina. Its mainland reaches just 274 miles from north to south, yet its coastline measures nearly 6,200 miles. For about a thousand years, the Celtic society here in the Highlands was built around the clan system; all the members of a clan bore the name of their chief and wore distinctive checkered wool cloth that would later be called tartan. The clans were broken up by England after 1746, when Bonnie Prince Charlie's attempt on the British crown was defeated. All clan lands were forfeited to the Crown, and the wearing of tartan and the playing of bagpipes were banned.

When the clan system ended, landowners began demanding rent from their tenants, most of whom could not pay it. Gradually the land was bought by farmers from England and southern Scotland, and in 1792, "the year of the sheep," thousands of tenants were evicted to make way for livestock.

Clare Nancy Macpherson-Grant, Laird of Ballindalloch, welcomes visitors from the Royal Scotsman *to the grounds of her home. An ancestor began building here early in the 16th century, and the laird's family has lived here ever since.*

Dinghies and reflected clouds share a mooring in Loch Awe. The long, thin Scottish lochs—or lakes—dot the countryside. Loch Lomond features in a popular sentimental folk song, and Loch Ness may harbor the enigmatic and elusive Nessie.

PRECEDING PAGES: "The most photographed castle in Scotland," Eilean Donan rises dramatically at the end of its causeway. Though occupation of the site dates from the late 6th or early 7th century, the castle is largely a 20th-century construction.

Many immigrated to Australia, Canada, and the United States. This period is known as "the clearances" and still is resented by many.

Today, more than half the inhabitants of the Highlands live in communities of fewer than a thousand people. The region was popularized by the writings of Sir Walter Scott and also by Queen Victoria, who loved northern Scotland and visited Balmoral here frequently, purchasing the estate in 1852.

Of the Highlands, D.H. Lawrence wrote, "There is still something of an Odyssey up there, in among the islands and the silent Lochs: like the twilight morning of the world, the herons fishing undisturbed by the water, and the sea running far in, for miles, between the wet trickling hills, where the cottages are low and almost invisible, built into the earth." English poet Thomas Gray called the Highland mountains "extatic."

But it's dinnertime again, and tonight the tables are lit with candles, the women are in long dresses, and the men in tuxedos. Fennel and lemon salad, roast loin of lamb, tartlet of tayberries. I sit with Al and Susan; he looks fine in his new jacket and a borrowed tie. He's probably the nicest person on the train, and I worry that he feels self-conscious. We talk about the wonderful British accent of the laird, about exchange students, about the art of packing, about band trips in high school. And about the scams Little Caesar customers try to run: They call and claim they've been made ill by a pizza but always are willing to settle for a coupon for a free pizza.

≡⊳◆⊲≡

IN THE MORNING, WE'RE UP EARLY FOR A 7 A.M. BREAKFAST, FOR WE HAVE A BUSY day ahead of us. The train moves at 8:10, through banks of heather and thin birches.

Our destination today is an unusual and interesting one: the Highland Wildlife Park, 260 acres devoted to animals indigenous to Scotland, including some that are either threatened or extinct in the wild.

With the senator's wife grumbling—"Why does the bus have to park so far from the entrance?"—we're greeted by Jeremy Usher Smith, park manager, trim and fit in a short-sleeved shirt, with a closely cropped beard. He welcomes us and escorts us to the vehicle that will take us around the park. To reach it, we must all walk through a footbath to disinfect our shoes: The foot-and-mouth outbreak hasn't reached Scotland, but precautions must be taken. A number of the hoofed species in the park would be at risk.

We drive at a crawl through the park and watch the animals watching us. Some sprawl on sunny hillsides; others nibble at grasses. We pass through a herd of European bison, "slightly larger than their American cousins," says Jeremy, to a chorus of American "N-o-os." Jeremy adds,

"These are descendants of 12 that were in captivity when the bison became extinct in the wild in 1919. They're the same animals as those seen in cave paintings in southern France."

Wolves doze in the sun. Scotland's last wild wolf was killed to the north of here in 1743. We drive among a small group of Przewalski's horses, the rarest animal in the park. "Their last stronghold was in Mongolia," says Jeremy. "They were extinct in the wild until recently, though there are about 1,400 in captivity worldwide. The park is holding this small group of stallions as a reserve stud group. Recently, people in Mongolia have supported the idea of restoring the horse there, and three herds have been released in a national park."

In a couple of large pens, big black turkey-size birds peck and scratch. "The males' song, as heard in the forest, is similar to the clip-clop of horses' hooves," says Jeremy." "The bird's name is derived from two Gaelic words—*capul collie*, meaning 'horse of the woods'." The capercaillie is dive-bombing toward extinction," says Jeremy. All the usual reasons: loss or degradation of habitat, overhunting, fence collisions by young birds, interruptions in feeding caused by mountain bikers and cross-country skiers. "

We rejoin the train at Kingussie about noon and head north toward Inverness, the capital of the Highlands; there we'll turn west toward Kyle of Lochalsh on perhaps the most scenic route in Britain. The track was laid in the late 1800s through countryside where some of the cuttings were nearly 90 feet deep. At Dingwall, given its name by the Norsemen, survive ruins of a castle where, they say, Macbeth was born.

Trains came to Scotland in the first half of the 19th century. In 1842 a line opened between Edinburgh and Glasgow, replacing an overnight canal-boat journey or a ride across the moors; by the early 1860s you could travel from Edinburgh to London in twelve and a half hours, though as the Scottish judge Lord Cockburn warned his daughter: "Only spines of steel could stand it." Thomas Cook's first Tartan Tours date from 1846.

In places our engine struggles as we climb hills. We pass through villages that consist of just a couple dozen houses: Gairbh, for instance. A picket fence, a few flowers, a highway, a train station. Shaggy cattle graze in the fields. We pass the Torridon Mountains, so old they contain no fossils. In the observation car the senator is asleep in a corner, and Pat has her feet up on a sofa, resting her rickety knees.

Infinitely patient, Marilyn is reassuring a couple of the most troublesome passengers—a retired American attorney and his wife, from Palm Springs, California—that she cares about their complaints. They're protesting that some of the other passengers have cabins closer to the dining cars than they do. "I just want what's comin' to me," he says. It occurs to me

Wielding floral fairy wands, bridesmaids pose at a wedding at the Trossachs Church at Loch Achray. The piper played before the ceremony but stopped when the bride appeared, a traditional Scottish signal of her arrival.

PRECEDING PAGES:
Hoary with age, headstones in a cemetery in Achanalt witness the passing Scotsman. Of working in Scotland, photographer Tino Soriano says, "Because it rains so much, the Scottish landscape can change dramatically in just a few minutes."

that, if it's true that youth is wasted on the young, perhaps it's also true that wealth is wasted on the rich.

We have fresh pasta with wild mushrooms and apple and blueberry crumble for lunch. I sit with "the Captain" and his wife. He's recovering from a stroke so has lost some of his alertness. His wife, however, easily into

her 80s, is salty and sharp. She was born in Bermuda and has lived there all her life. Her ancestors were shipwrecked in 1694. "They lost their ship but found Bermuda," she says. She met her husband during the Cold War. He was captain of a U.S. Navy vessel, and she was in charge of assigning berths in the harbor. He didn't like the berth he was given, and complained. She told him, "If you don't like it here you can go to hell, and I'll supply the tugs." They've been married 39 years.

Late in the afternoon we disembark in the village of Plockton for more animals, seals this time, in the harbor. A little boat captained by Calum Mackenzie takes us bobbing gently out into the picturesque harbor where, sure enough, sleek seals on wave-washed rocks look up from their naps with shy, cowlike eyes as we pass. Captain Mackenzie almost got in trouble some

Formally dressed passengers enjoy a whiskey in the observation car before dining. Two dinners aboard the train are billed as black tie, and passengers dress accordingly. The Royal Scotsman *has been running in its current configuration since 1990.*

time back because he *guarantees* in his brochure that visitors will see seals. This caused some joking in Plockton that he must have an army of plastic seals ready to sprinkle about if need be. The gibe got back to the Scottish equivalent of the truth-in-advertising people and officials arrived to check him out. Plockton's Main Street runs alongside the harbor and is almost eerily peaceful as we stroll back to our bus.

On the train, stabled at Kyle of Lochalsh, I sit in the observation car reading *Rob Roy* by Sir Walter Scott. A little bird with a red breast sits on a fence by the track and sings through my open window. Marilyn comes upon me reading and expresses some surprise. "You know, don't you, that you're the only person in Scotland reading Sir Walter Scott?" I'm enjoying the book, though when Scott turns on the dialect I'm pretty well lost. I read, "Am trenching up the sparry-grass, and am gaun to saw sum Misegun beans; they winna want them to their swine's flesh, I'se warrant—muckle gude may it do them."

After another black-tie dinner—terrine of seasonal fruits, cumin-scented monkfish with risotto, crème brûlée with strawberries—Mary Strachan from the Isle of Skye sings in the observation car, accompanying herself on a *clarsach,* or small harp. Her songs are in Gaelic, a language slowly making a comeback. About 50,000 Scots currently speak the language, and several of the train stations we've passed through have the town's name both in English and in Gaelic.

FRIDAY, OUR LAST FULL DAY ON THE TRAIN, STARTS WITH A BIG BREAKFAST—THE chef does perfect scrambled eggs—carries through more field trips, and ends with black angus steaks and a tucked-in teddy bear.

By bus, we swing by Eilean Donan Castle, the most photographed castle in Scotland. It sits on a rocky promontory where three sea lochs meet and indeed begs to be photographed. Its origins date back to prehistory, though a castle probably was not built here until the early 13th century as a defensive measure against the Vikings.

"When King James II of England was deposed in 1689," says Marilyn, trying to teach us a little of Scotland's complex history, "his supporters, the Jacobites—which is from the Latin for James—made various attempts to put him, his son, or subsequently his grandson, Bonnie Prince Charlie, back onto the throne. In the late spring of 1719, the castle was a Jacobite garrison, and on May 10, three government frigates sailed into Loch Duich. The bombardment and explosion of 343 barrels of gunpowder in the magazine reduced the place to rubble and the ruins lay neglected for nearly two centuries."

It was bought by John MacRae-Gilstrap in 1911 and completely rebuilt by 1932. Today it stands proudly on its site, so perfect it might be a movie

With typically Scottish face and demeanor, ticket taker John Royale
checks passengers aboard the Strathspey Railway, *a tourist train
that runs between Aviemore and Boat of Garten.*

OPPOSITE: *As dusk falls, Scotland recedes from the rear of the train.
The train pauses every day so passengers can make various
excursions by bus—including trips to a couple of castles, a game park,
and a distillery.*

set, and in fact it shows up in movies and TV shows. Sean Connery was filmed here for *Highlander,* and in 1999 James Bond made a visit.

In the banqueting hall, plump and cheery Agnes, with a lovely Glasgow accent, tells us about the castle and points out a lock of Bonnie Prince Charlie's hair in a glass case. In the gift shop I buy a map of the Scottish Highlands, and when the middle-aged saleswoman hands me my change, she says, "There you are, my treasure."

From Eilean Donan the bus takes us on a beautiful drive to the Isle of Skye, one of the Inner Hebrides islands off the northwest coast of Scotland. It's just 670 square miles, full of sheep and cattle and famed for its wild, mountainous scenery. We pass ancient stone walls, thatched roofs, waterfalls, fish farms, neat houses in neat villages. Even the rugged mountains look somehow neat, as if they've been tended by landscapers. Because of the numerous sea lochs, a visitor is never more than five miles from the ocean. Samuel Johnson, in his *Journey to the Western Islands of Scotland,* wrote of Skye: "Their winter overtakes their summer, and their harvest lies upon the ground drenched with rain." Poor Bonnie Prince Charlie, on the run, escaped to Skye in 1746, disguised as the maidservant of a woman called Flora Macdonald, whose grave is here. She was buried wrapped in a sheet taken from his bed.

Today, when we arrive back at the train, Camilla and Alan greet us with trays of Bloody Marys, which taste good on such a chilly day.

No trip to Scotland would be complete without a taste of Scotch whiskey, so while we lunch on the train—chicken and langoustine salad and raspberry cheesecake—we retrace some of our route, pass through Inverness, and head down the east side of the Highlands to Keith. Here the Strathisla Distillery, the oldest operating distillery in the Scottish Highlands, maintains traditions and techniques laid down more than 200 years ago.

We tour the distillery and are dazzled by the complexity of whiskey making; I wonder how anyone ever thought of it in the first place. As the salmon smokehouse smelled of fish, the distillery smells of…I guess, malted barley. We emerge at the end and are rewarded by a tumbler with a finger of Scotch in it, which I down with difficulty, not being a Scotch drinker, and pass through the inevitable gift shop.

Back aboard the train, we rumble south through an agricultural area to

PRECEDING PAGES: *In a thundering blur, the* Royal Scotsman *passes by. Passengers prize its luxury, its attentive staff, and its leisurely route through the romantic Highlands of Scotland.*

Aberdeen, the Granite City, then follow the coast through Stonehaven, Montrose, and Carnoustie on our way to Dundee, where we will park for the night.

Tonight's dinner—hot smoked salmon with potato remoulade, fillet of Aberdeen Angus with red wine jus, prune and Armagnac soufflé—is informal, the men in sport coats and ties. I sit with Pat, the California writer, her granddaughter Rachel, and Marilyn. Pat bristles when someone suggests that writing must be an interesting hobby. "I am an author," she says. "That is my job. I write for a living. As Mr. Johnson said, 'No man but a blockhead ever wrote except for money.' "

Marilyn confesses she lost a filling from a tooth early on our trip but has concealed it from the passengers. "It doesn't hurt," she protests. "It just feels funny." Still, she wins praise for quietly soldiering on.

Pat did much of her early work as a television garden-show host in California, emphasizing the things you should or could do in the different seasons. Also, she's written columns about gardening for various publications, as well as books. Hers is a strong personality that has rubbed some of the passengers the wrong way, but I find her interesting. And everyone loves Rachel, her very mature yet teenage granddaughter. Rachel has brought a teddy bear on the trip, and every evening while we're at dinner the girls who make up the cabins for the night have been arranging teddy in various poses. Tonight when Rachel goes to bed she finds him propped up in bed, a book in his lap, a reading visor on his head, and a wineglass and some chocolates nearby.

Our last morning goes by quickly, a short run from Dundee to Edinburgh. We cross the Firth of Forth on the Forth Railway Bridge. It was considered one of the great engineering achievements of the Victorian Age. The English travel writer Henry Morton wrote, in 1929, "To see the Forth Bridge is rather like meeting a popular actress, but with this difference; it exceeds expectations." The first major steel-built bridge in the world, it opened in 1890.

And Edinburgh is upon us. Castle Rock here has been occupied since about 1000 B.C., and the city's oldest building, St. Margaret's Chapel, which dates from the 11th century, is here. Here also, in a 15th-century palace, Mary Queen of Scots gave birth to James VI, who became James I of England.

The train drops us in Waverley Station, just off Princes Street, and suddenly we're saying our good-byes. Good-bye Pat and Rachel, good-bye senator, good-bye Don and Phoebe, good-bye Germans, good-bye Al and Susan. Good-bye Marilyn.

By the time I get off the train, my luggage, always one step ahead of me when it's in the hands of the *Royal Scotsman,* is already deposited in a waiting taxi.

A person could get used to service like that.

THE EASTERN
& ORIENTAL
EXPRESS

By Phil Macdonald

Photos by
Chris Anderson

"Welcome to Malaysia" says the sign at Keppel Road Station. But this is not Malaysia.

This is Singapore: A prosperous, orderly, and polished speck of an island nuzzling the tip of the string-bean Malay Peninsula and home to four million comfortably well-off souls. A more rough and ready Malaysia is down the track, about 40 minutes north. First I have to board the luxurious *Eastern & Oriental Express*, roll along 15 miles of railway line, slip across the half-mile causeway bridging the narrow Strait of Johor, and then I am in Malaysia. Well, I'm almost right. Thanks to a little historical irony, it seems once I have arrived at Singapore's Keppel Road Station, I have arrived in Malaysia.

The station, just south of the gleaming high-rises of Singapore's downtown, is owned and operated by Keretapi Tanah Melayu, or more simply KTM, Malaysia's government railway system. The station's ownership is a throwback to more tumultuous times of the 1960s, when Singapore, after earlier gaining independence from Britain in 1959, was incorporated into the Malaysian Federation. But the union did not last long. Consummated on August 31, 1963, it was torn apart two years later, when Malaysia decided it no longer wanted its inconsolable neighbor (although it seems it wanted to keep its railway station).

Although spartan and somewhat neglected, Keppel Road Station has a certain presumption about it. After all it was the British, whose penchant for building grand railway stations in its Southeast Asia colonies bordered on the neurotic, who built it.

Inside, a half dozen colorful murals rise to the high ceiling—motifs romanticizing Malaysian life. On one, sarong-clad men clamber up coconut palms; another celebrates seafaring ways with clippers, sampans, Chinese

PRECEDING PAGES: *The railway station at the seaside resort of Hua Hin is one of the most quaint and colorful in Thailand. The town, about 140 miles south of Bangkok, became a favorite haunt of royalty and the Thai elite in the early decades of the 20th century.*

junks, and coolies lugging boxes ashore; on the third, village life is portrayed with images of thatched homes on stilts, industrious villagers, and water buffalo hauling wagons. On others workers tap rubber trees, farmers till rice fields, and muscular men carry wicker baskets of tin ore from open-cut mines.

The only train on the platforms on this Wednesday morning is the *Eastern & Oriental Express*, readying itself for a journey that will take me and 72 other passengers 1,262 miles along the Malay Peninsula through Malaysia and Thailand to clamorous Bangkok in 41 hours. Its 13 sleepers, one presidential car, two restaurant cars, one bar car, one lounge car, one power car, one observation car, and two staff cars will be hauled by locomotives at a sedate speed made necessary by the narrow 1,000-millimeter gauge track, a slimness that promises its fair share of swaying, jolts, and lunges.

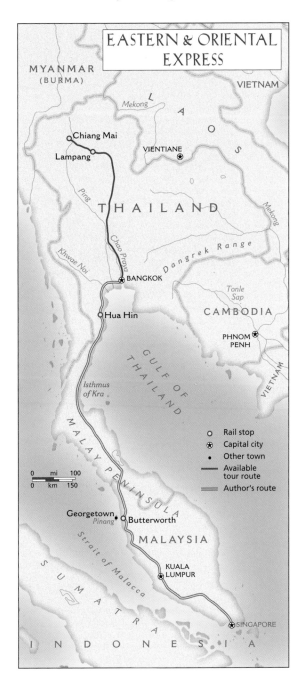

We are promised luxurious private cabins, impeccable, unobtrusive service, and gourmet food. We will be cocooned in five-star splendor as we glimpse the backyards of three countries. We'll roll past vast rubber and palm-oil plantations, through picturesque villages and bustling towns with gold-domed mosques and flamboyant Buddhist temples, cut through fiery emerald green rice fields that spread to distant jungle-clad mountain ranges, and rumble past seaside holiday towns and giant limestone cliffs erupting from plantations of pineapples and bananas.

I can't wait.

After handing over our tickets and being assigned our compartments, we are shepherded through Malaysian immigration. (Another quirk of having your train station in a different country is that passengers are processed into Malaysia before being stamped out of Singapore. Our official exit from

Singapore does not happen for another half hour or so when we are bundled off the train at suburban Woodlands immigration checkpoint.) The gleaming *Eastern & Oriental Express* takes up the length of the platform, looking suitably impressive. Its corrugated sides are painted in shiny British "racing green" with a beige strip and white roof. On each carriage the train's name is embossed with shiny brass lettering along with its crest—a circular emblem in gold lettering with a sleek tiger prancing above it.

Staff, wearing colorful batik vests over crisp white shirts, stand at the entrance to each car checking tickets and pointing us in the right direction. I end up in the front of car D and Songkrom, the car's steward. Songkrom, like most of the train staff, comes from Thailand. He exhibits that easygoing and helpful demeanor intrinsic to the Thai personality. He presents

Passengers enjoy a fine dinner in one of the opulent dining cars of the Eastern & Oriental Express. *Table d'hôte meals are of consistent excellence; gracious service and beautifully decorated cars make for a splendid dining experience.*

himself with a traditional *wai*; palms pressed together and head slightly bowed. I get to see Songkrom many times over the next couple of days; the smile never disappears from his face. He shows me to my compartment and promises he'll be back soon to make sure I'm comfortable. One look at the compartment tells me that won't be too difficult.

The train's director of passenger services, Ulf Buchert, tells me later that the inspiration for the interior design of the train is forged in celluloid. My cabin's diamond-shaped wood marquetry and antique-style brass fittings are similar to Shanghai Lily's compartment on the *Shanghai Express* in the 1932 movie of the same name, starring Marlene Dietrich at her vampish best. Dietrich ("It took more than one man to change my name to Shanghai Lily") is a notorious adventuress and a lady of questionable reputation, making the journey from Peking to Shanghai. In the hectic opening scene full of jostling crowds, plumes of steam, piercing whistles, and scurrying porters, the train readies for its journey north to Shanghai while civil war rages throughout China. One of the train's passengers, Reverend Carmichael (Lawrence Grant), complains to fellow passenger British Medical Corps Capt. Donald Harvey (Clive Brook) about the women traveling on the train: "Well, sir, I suppose every train carries its cargo of sin, but this train is burdened with more than its share."

Our departure from Keppel Station is far more subdued than Lily's. Ten minutes after boarding, the *Eastern & Oriental Express* lurches away from the empty platform, and my smile is as wide as Songkrom's.

I have already settled into the cozy opulence of my cabin, hitched the window curtains apart, pulled forward the leg rest, and nestled into the corner of the plush sofa by the window to take in the views. Not that there is much to see at this stage; a freeway running parallel to the tracks, thin with traffic; tall grass, bamboo, and scruffy vegetation lining the tracks; multistory housing estates, warehouses, factories; and the occasional vegetable garden. Songkrom returns and gives me a quick tour of the cabin, opening and closing doors, flicking light switches on and off, adjusting the air-conditioning, demonstrating how to work the hot- and cold-water taps in the shower stall in the bathroom, and pointing out no end of the nooks and crannies this ingeniously designed little cabin harbors. He shows me the switch that sounds a buzzer and ignites a red light on the outside of the cabin and invites me to use it to summon him if I need anything to make my journey more comfortable.

After 30 minutes we arrive at Woodlands and are rushed through immigration, then planted back on the train. The first sitting for lunch is called—there are two sittings for meals—as we roll over the traffic-clogged causeway that separates Singapore from the Malaysian city of Johor Baharu.

Modern Singapore still contains many reminders of its past, such as its historic Chinatown district, a vibrant area of renovated shop-houses and bustling mercantilism.

FOLLOWING PAGES:
The high-rises of Singapore's financial district form a glittering backdrop for a bride's wedding photos. From a scruffy backwater in 1819, the city-state grew to become one of Asia's financial and business hubs.

Johor Baharu feeds off the affluence of Singapore. Singaporean industrialists built their factories here to take advantage of cheaper labor, and on weekends the city's shopping centers are filled with Singaporeans picking up goods at bargain prices. On the city's outskirts, clutches of all-but-completed 20-story apartment buildings rising out of cleared jungle stand as a void between boom and bust brought on by the Asian economic crisis of 1997-99.

Not far out of the city the first of the palm-oil plantations appears at the track's edge, rising and falling on the surrounding hillsides. The sharply serrated fronds on these trees shelter thick clusters of red nuts that, when pressed, produce oil. Much of southern Malaysia is carpeted by vast estates of these palms, producing six million tons of oil a year. Malaysia is the world's biggest producer of palm oil. Just as the train starts to pick up some momentum, it suddenly slows and eases to a halt at a small railway station called Kulai. A uniformed guard stands on the lonely platform waving a red flag. It's 12:35 p.m., and we are about one and a half hours into our journey. Our 25-minute wait at Kulai is one of many enforced intervals along the route, made to allow other trains coming in the opposite direction to pass.

We pass small villages with wooden homes with rusty corrugated iron roofs and messy backyards—some with waddling ducks and ponds—edging the tracks. In one backyard I see a monkey on a chain perched on the roof of a shed, casually watching the train rush by. Occasionally the white minarets of a village mosque poke above groves of banana trees. In one village, porcelain figurines of dragons, gargoyles, and other mythical creatures line the roof ridges of a Chinese Taoist temple. At road intersections, people on motorcycles and bicycles wait patiently behind a barrier as our train passes. The women wear blazingly colorful floral and batik head scarves in deference to their Muslim faith.

Past Kluang, about two hours and 70 miles out of Singapore, regimented rows of silver-bark rubber trees now share the countryside with the oil palms. Each rubber tree is cut by a diagonal gash, with a small bowl affixed to catch the white latex oozing from the trunk. Malaysia is the world's third largest producer of rubber.

At 1:45 p.m., a voice comes over the intercom in my cabin, announcing himself as the mâitre d' and inviting us to the second lunch seating.

I head down the narrow corridors of the carriages toward one of two dining cars—this one is called the Singapura, looking suitably Chinese with a rosewood veneer and delicate flowers painted on lacquered panels. I occasionally need to turn sideways to shimmy past passengers and staff heading in the opposite direction. I dine on shrimp and pomelo salad infused with Asian spices, chicken in fragrant turmeric with tomato and onion sauce, and mango and passion fruit parfait served with orange tuile. Rain splats against the window, and the swaying and occasional jolts of the train make diners grab for their crystal wine glasses out of fear they will tip and spill. Throughout the trip our three-course table d'hôte meals are consistently fine and impeccably presented. The cuisine on board typically blends Asian and European ingredients, but holds out on the more fiery Asian traits. All this

surprising largesse comes from two galley kitchens just twenty-six feet long and six and a half feet wide, with a gangway of two feet between the two banks of kitchen equipment and a half dozen chefs.

After lunch I settle down in the saloon carriage. Director of Passenger Services Buchert tells me that the train, when hauling its maximum 22 carriages, holds 132 guests. On this trip there are 73 of us, and we come from all over the place. There are Americans, Canadians, Australians, Portuguese, Germans, Swiss, British, Japanese, Mexicans, Puerto Ricans, and Singaporeans. Americans, Buchert tells me, make up the bulk of *Eastern & Oriental Express* passengers. In any year 26 percent of passengers will come from the United States.

In 1977, millionaire hotel and sea-container magnate James B. Sherwood began buying up and restoring original Pullman and wagon-lit

Cuisine aboard marries European and Asian ingredients into imaginative and impeccably presented dishes, although it tends to go easy on the more spicy traits of the East in deference to the tastes of mainly Western passengers.

A tower and cupola rise above the Eastern & Oriental Express *at Kuala Lumpur Station. The station, completed in 1910, is a whimsical architectural adventure of Moorish-inspired minarets, cupolas, colonnades, and arches.*

The open-air observation car at the rear of the
train allows you to catch the scenery and cool
breezes. The best time to head here is at sunrise,
when a veil of mist evaporates under a rising sun
to reveal Southeast Asia beginning a new day.

A farmer and his children make their way
through a field on a motorbike in the Pinang
countryside. Small motorbikes are popular
with poorer families in rural Malaysia, and it
is not unusual to see Dad, Mum, and a
couple of kids aboard.

RIGHT: Curving trunks of coconut palms rise
under a leaden sky in rural Pinang. Deep,
vibrant shades of green, from tall grasses,
tangled vines, and jungle foliage to palm
plantations and emerald rice fields, dominate
the countryside throughout most of the trip.

carriages, which were scattered all over Europe, to reincarnate the legendary *Venice Simplon-Orient-Express*. Little more than four years later Sherwood had managed to put together enough train to start a service. On May 25, 1982, the *Venice Simplon-Orient-Express* left on its inaugural run from London to Venice. The thought of a similar travel experience through Southeast Asia was probably not far from his mind when Sherwood and his wife, Shirley, climbed aboard a KTM train at Singapore's Keppel Station bound for Bangkok in 1987. By the time Sherwood reached Bangkok, he was convinced a luxury train service rolling through three Southeast Asian countries would appeal to travelers. The region has no legacy of luxury train travel as in Europe; there were no once grand, dilapidated Pullmans or wagons-lits sitting in desultory railway yards in this part of the world. Sherwood had to start from scratch.

This time he purchased 24 stainless steel-bodied carriages that operated as the *Silver Star* in New Zealand. The carriages were stripped to their shells, brakes overhauled, and bogies re-gauged to fit the narrow track widths of Malaysia and Thailand before being shipped to Singapore. Sherwood brought back the team responsible for the restoration of the *Venice Simplon-Orient-Express,* French decorator Gerard Gallet and James Park Associates in London. On September 19, 1993, the *Eastern & Oriental Express* heaved out of Keppel Station on its first journey to Bangkok. Surprisingly, the *Eastern & Oriental Express* became the first train along this route to offer passengers a direct service from Singapore to Bangkok. Passengers on trains from Thailand and Singapore still have to swap trains at Butterworth in Pinang, Malaysia.

Unlike its sister in Europe, a sense of history—and indeed mystery—is missing from the *Eastern & Oriental Express*. It has no predecessor. It is no reincarnation. The train is designed to evoke luxury travel of the 1920s and 1930s—down to the art deco posters available in the gift shop—although trains in Southeast Asia have always been utilitarian beasts, more intent on carting people from point A to point B than laying on style. One could dismiss the train as contrived. It sets up an illusion of what train travel should have been like in this part of the world, rather than what it was like. Still, even in the dourest moments of cynicism, it's hard not to be impressed by the five-star camouflage.

Trains came to Malaysia and Thailand in the later part of the 19th century. The Sultan of Johor built Malaysia's first track in 1869, constructed completely from wood. Ants made short work of it. Britain, the colonial power, brought in engineers to help with construction. Chinese, Malay, and Javanese workers cut through thick jungles and laid tracks hauled into place by elephants and bullocks. By 1885 a line—this time using steel—was opened between Taiping, the center of the country's lucrative tin-mining industry, and Port Weld, eight miles away on the west coast of the peninsula. A year later a link was established to Kuala Lumpur. By 1909, trains traveled along lines 250 miles north to Pinang and south to Seremban and on to Johor at the tip of the peninsula. In 1910, the magnificent Moorish-style railway station in Kuala Lumpur, the Malaysian capital, was built as the hub of a rail network spreading throughout the country.

Meanwhile Thailand, using clever diplomacy, had managed to stave off the colonial expansion, but at the same time its progressive kings embraced modernization. In 1890, King Chulalongkorn (Rama V) created the Royal State Railways of Siam. The first line was built between Bangkok and Park Nam at the mouth of the Chao Phraya River, 16 miles south. Another line north from Bangkok to the old capital of Ayutthaya was built in 1897, followed by another line to the seaside town of Hua Hin, 120 miles south. By 1918, the Thai and Malaysian rail networks met at the border town of Padang Besar. The completion of the causeway linking Singapore to the mainland in 1923 meant it was possible to travel by train from Bangkok to Singapore, a journey that took 60 hours.

By late afternoon, the train is rolling past plantations of bananas, oil and coconut palms, and towns with crisp names: Tampin, Tebong, and Rembau. On land that has not been cleared by the plantation owners, relentless creepers spread from the edge of the tracks and wrap themselves around bushes and trees. Trackside streams full of pink and white lotus flowers add a splash of contrast to the intense green of the countryside. As we draw closer to Kuala Lumpur, towns become more frequent and more modern. Streets lined with tidy new homes appear, along with shopping malls and high-rise apartment buildings. We arrive at the magnificent Kuala Lumpur Railway Station just after sunset to the haunting sounds of Muslim prayers broadcast through loudspeakers from nearby mosques.

The Kuala Lumpur Railway Station embraces Islamic-Moorish architecture with a fantasy of spires, minarets, cupolas, colonnades, and arches. Beneath this whimsical exterior it is similar to glass-and-iron railway stations built in Britain during the Victorian era. It is said that construction of the station was held up because the original roof design did not meet British railway specifications. Pith-helmeted British engineers, sweating under the tropical sun, decided it had to be sturdy enough to support one meter of snow.

In 1857, 87 Chinese prospectors sailed up the Kelang River by raft to where it converges with the Gombak River. The prospectors cut their way through dense jungle, finally stumbling across rich deposits of tin. Within two years a trading post was set up at the confluence of the two rivers in what is now the middle of Kuala Lumpur (the name comes from the Malay

Rambutans are displayed at an open-air market in Pinang. The tough, hairy red skin of the rambutan easily peels open to a delicious, translucent, fleshy fruit. Malaysians often brag that their rambutans are the best in Southeast Asia.

FOLLOWING PAGES: *Passengers enjoy a Thai traditional dance in the bar carriage before dinner. The gilded costume, darting eyes, and sublime hand movements of the dancer are captivating.*

A trishaw (bicycle rickshaw) driver in George Town, Pinang, catches
a nap between passengers. George Town has a large fleet of trishaws,
which these days are more popular with tourists out for a leisurely
ride around the city than they are with locals.

for "muddy confluence"). Tin ore was shipped downriver to the port city of Kelang. After a spluttering start, Kuala Lumpur grew into a brawling, noisy boomtown that eventually tempered and prospered under the rule of the British. By 1895, it had become the capital of the Federated Malay States. By the time the grandiose Kuala Lumpur Railway Station was built, the city had a population of more than 40,000. Today, about 1.5 million people live in this modern cosmopolitan capital. Its signature landmark, the gleaming pinnacles of the 88-story Petronas Twin Towers at 1,482 feet are the tallest buildings in the world.

At 8:10 p.m., a train horn blasts and we crawl out of Kuala Lumpur. I make my way down the narrow swaying corridors of the train for dinner. Like lunch it is a delight: Fricassee of asparagus lobster with Siamese risotto for starters; followed by Australian lamb in massaman sauce and compote of tomato; and finished with ricotta and almond gateau and honey ice cream, coffee, and petits fours. After dinner I head to the Bar Carriage for a nightcap. Things are quiet. A few couples are clasping drinks and listening to a pony-tailed pianist, dressed in a tuxedo, playing easy-on-the-ear tunes.

When I return to my cabin, Songkrom has transformed the sofa into a bed. I crawl between crisp linen sheets.

<hr />

I AWAKE AT 6:30 A.M. AND IT'S STILL DARK. I RING THE SERVICE BELL AND AFTER A discreet knock, Songkrom appears asking me if I'd like breakfast. He brings a tray of coffee, strawberry yogurt, warm bread rolls, croissants, jams, Danish pastries, and little chunks of melon. I eat hurriedly because I want to catch the sunrise from the observation car at the back. In Southeast Asia, this is the finest moment of the day.

The cool, moist air rushing through the open-sided teak-paneled car leaves a tingle on my face and arms. The heavy morning mist evaporates under the rising sun, gently unveiling wooden stilt houses, palms, and banana groves. We roll through a morning alive with activity. Women tend vegetable gardens and scatter feed for ducks in their backyards. Boys play early morning soccer on barren playing fields between rusty goal posts. Under trees, groups move in unison while practicing *tai ji quan*. People heading off to work on motorcycles (and children off to school on bicycles) bunch up at intersections watching the train pass. The men waiting on their bikes wear their light jackets the wrong way around (a curiosity you find throughout Singapore and Malaysia).

We arrive at Butterworth mid-morning and are unloaded onto two buses for a ferry trip across to the island of Pinang, known as Pulau Pinang or Betel Nut Island in Malay. It is the oldest British settlement in Malaysia, dating back to 1786 when Capt. Francis Light took possession on behalf of the British East India Company. The island, with its soft-sanded beaches, rugged, mountainous hinterland, and charming capital of George Town, is

a favorite holiday destination. While we are waiting on the bus for the ferry, our guide, a young Malaysian Chinese, reels off facts and figures on Malaysia and Pinang, enthusiastically pointing at two souvenir-style dishcloth maps hanging in front of the driver, one decorated with a map of Malaysia, the other with a map of Pinang.

Pinang is shaped like a turtle, she tells us, although I'm thinking it's shaped more like a frog. She tells us the country is made up of 58 percent *Bumiputra*, or "sons of the soil" (Malays and indigenous groups); 27 percent Chinese; and 8 percent Indian. We get a primer on Muslim *Sharia* law—how an unmarried couple cannot be alone in private and how Muslim women cannot enter beauty contests.

George Town is a delightful amalgam of Chinese, Malay, and Indian

A hawker treads the sands of Hua Hin beach, south of Bangkok.
Once the playground of wealthy Thai, Hua Hin is now becoming
popular with foreign tourists as the luxury hotels strung along its
beachfront attest.

Buddhist monks pray at Wat Pho temple in Bangkok. About 95 percent of Thai are Theravada Buddhist. The religion is an intrinsic part of Thai culture, dominating many aspects of daily life.

OPPOSITE: *Richly ornate* chedis *at Wat Pho are typical of the flamboyance of Thai temple architecture. Wat Pho, one of Bangkok's most important temple compounds, has a wonderful collection of religious structures.*

PRECEDING PAGES: *Bustling up and down narrow canals, vendors sell fresh produce from small boats at Damnoen Saduak Floating Market, some 60 miles southwest of Bangkok. While the remaining floating markets in Bangkok are little more than tourist shows, Damnoen Saduak is the real thing.*

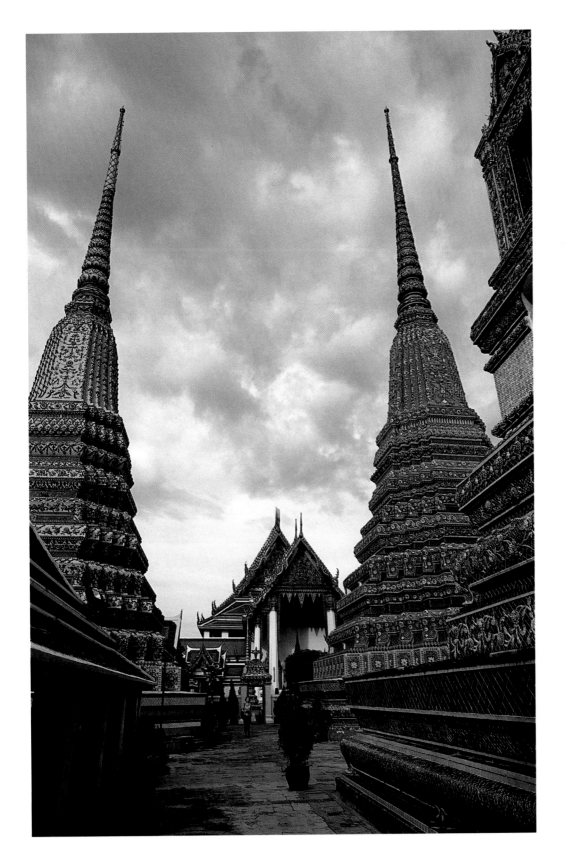

culture blended with colonial architecture. Parts of the center of the city have been restored. Spruced, verandaed Chinese shop-houses, known as "five-foot-aways" because when built the doorways had to be a uniform five feet away from the road, line clean, narrow streets. We dutifully hop off the bus in the center of town near a shabby side street dubiously called Love Lane and are herded into a busy market where vendors sell rambutans, durians, jackfruits, mustard seed and chilies, Chinese herbs, fish, and shrimp. Waiting for us around the corner is a flotilla of trishaws (bicycle rickshaws), each shaded with a British racing green umbrella emblazoned with the *Eastern & Oriental Express* logo.

We climb aboard, and 50 or so trishaws manned by mostly sun-wizened elderly Chinese pedalers head off in a surreal cavalry charge around the streets of Pinang. First we pedal to Little India, where high-pitched Hindu music blares out from shops selling spices, bolts of silk and satin, and finely spun gold jewelry. On Queen Street, Hindu holy men with long beards and matted hair emerge from the elaborately sculptured *gopuram*, the pyramidal gateway tower soaring over the entrance to Sri Mariamman Temple. We wind our way through the narrow streets past Chinese shop-houses with heavy timber doors and shuttered windows before cutting onto a busy road and past the wonderfully restored Eastern and Oriental Hotel, built in 1885 and one of the oldest hotels operating in Southeast Asia. Along the Esplanade we head past the timeworn walls of Fort Cornwallis, built between 1808 and 1810 and one of Pinang's oldest sites, before arriving back at the ferry terminal.

We leave Butterworth at midday. After lunch I spend much of the afternoon on the open observation car. The section of the trip to the Thai border passes through the fertile plains of Kedah, a state that supplies Malaysia with more than half its rice crop, and some of the finest country-side so far. Here, the railway tracks unfold along hundreds upon hundreds of acres of brilliant green rice fields, running to the jagged mountain ranges in the distance. Stilted timber farmhouses set in the fields are partially hidden in groves of palm trees. As we rumble over small steel-girder bridges past quaint, all-but-deserted railway stations, I occasionally spot the gilded dome of a mosque in the distance. Closer to the Thai border giant limestone rocks hundreds of feet high erupt from rice fields. Some are shaped like loaves of bread, others jagged pinnacles, their ocher cliff faces partially covered with rich jungle foliage.

There is a 45-minute delay at the border town of Padang Besar where passports are checked, watches turned back one hour to sync with Thai time, and the train swaps locomotives. State Railways of Thailand locos will haul us through to Bangkok. Our new drivers appear to be a bit more free spirited than their Malaysian counterparts, and the train speeds up noticeably.

After dinner I once again head to the bar carriage. It is livelier than the previous night. Passengers are crowded into the carriage to watch a performance of traditional Thai dance, involving a lone female dancer wearing a dazzling gilded costume. Her darting eyes and exquisite hand movements captivate the audience. After the performance I order some beer and eavesdrop on conversations. After more than 35 hours aboard, people have lost their reserve and are chatting freely with one another. A Canadian woman talks loud and long about safaris in Africa to a small group. A friendly and effusive young couple from the United States, halfway through their honeymoon, join me. The *Eastern & Oriental Express* is part of their Asian adventure. They have been to Bali and Singapore. After Bangkok, they are heading to Hong Kong, then Japan before returning to the United States.

I AWAKE ON FRIDAY MORNING TO FIND THE TRAIN FOUR HOURS BEHIND SCHEDULE. The locomotive broke down during the evening, and we had to wait for a replacement to arrive. The delay proved fortuitous, because we now find ourselves amid the most beautiful scenery of the trip, sights we would have missed if the train had rumbled away through the night.

We are on the slender neck of undulating land connecting southern Thailand with Bangkok and the Central Plains, about 90 miles south of where we should be. A dozen or so miles to the west are wild mountains that mark the border with Myanmar, and just to the east is the Gulf of Thailand, in many places cut from view by enormous limestone cliffs that plunge into the gulf. As the cool, moist tropical morning air prickles the skin and enlivens the spirit, no one in the observation car is rankled about the delay. In the distance, we see the huge cliffs that buttress the sweeping bay at the sleepy fishing village of Prachnap Khiri Khan. Hundreds of shrimp farms, with rows of tiny waterwheels chugging across pools to aerate the water, line the railway tracks.

We gradually pull away from the coast and closer to the mountains of Myanmar. Here, gilded, steep-roofed, riotously ornate Buddhist temples rise amid rice paddies fringed by groves of palm and banana. The train then curves back toward the coast to meet Khao Sam Roi Yot ("mountain of three hundred peaks"), a range of limestone mountains whose peaks cut jagged patterns into the clear blue sky.

After more engine trouble that keeps us stalled on the tracks for about an hour, we glide into Hua Hin Railway Station at about 11:30 a.m. This

*Gilded mythical figures line a wall at Wat
Phra Kaeo. Wat Phra Kaeo and the Grand
Palace—consecrated in 1782, the year
Bangkok became the Thai capital—
encompass more than a hundred royal and
religious buildings.*

FOLLOWING PAGES: *A mosaic-encrusted yak
(mythical giant) figure guards a stupa at Wat
Phra Kaeo and the Grand Palace.
The dazzling brilliance, ornateness,
and extravagance of this place leaves
indelible memories.*

*The Golden Chedi at Wat Phra Kaeo within the Grand Palace
complex houses a sacred relic, a piece of Buddha's breastbone. The
chedi is just one example of the magnificence of Wat Phra Kaeo, one
of the wonders of Southeast Asia.*

historic seaside town was Thailand's first beach resort, attracting the leisure classes from Bangkok as long ago as the 1920s. The towns in this part of Thailand have long enjoyed the favor of Thai royalty. A special royal waiting room, done in the flamboyant style of a Thai temple, sits on the platform. Thai Chakri Dynasty kings and princes built teak palaces by the beach, sailed their yachts, and played golf. In 1932, while playing golf at the Royal Hua Hin Golf Course, the leisure-prone King Prajadhiphok (Rama VII) was told he had just been overthrown in a bloodless coup, abruptly ending 165 years of absolute monarchy and his golf game. Today's king, the revered King Bhumibol (Rama IX), finds time to holiday and sail his dinghies here.

At Phetchaburi, another 35 miles or so north along the track, we spot the magnificent Phra Nakhon Khiri built by King Mongkut (Rama IV) in 1859 perched majestically atop a 302-foot hill. This is where the avid astronomer Mongkut would view the constellations from his royal observatory. This complex of grand buildings includes a temple, an enormous spiraling *chedi*, and a neoclassical-style mansion, which now houses a museum full of dynastic opulence. Here the skies leaden, accentuating the deep emerald green rice fields. Rain spits against the windows of my cabin.

Instead of heading straight to Bangkok, the *Eastern & Oriental Express* cuts east through Thailand's central plains towards Myanmar. We reach Kanchanaburi late in the afternoon. Passengers are unloaded from the train before it slowly rolls onto the bridge made famous in the 1957 movie *Bridge on the River Kwai*, starring Alec Guinness and William Holden. Cameras click and whirl as passengers take photographs of the train as it pauses on the bridge. We board an enormous raft towed by a longtail boat for a trip under the bridge and down the Kwai River. A brochure left in our cabins the night before explains the terrible toll exacted by the building of the bridge and the 255-mile serpentine Thailand-Burma "Death" Railway during World War II:

> *Official Japanese figures state that the total POW labour force employed on the job was 68,888 and, in addition, some 200,000 Asian workers were "recruited" at a wage of one Straits dollar a day.... British records claim that 13,000 Australians, 30,000 British, 18,000 Dutch and 700 Americans worked on the railway and that more than 16,000 died on its construction.... at least 80,000-100,000 of the Asian labourers also died.*

We float past innumerable holiday boathouses and enormous floating discos docked on the banks of the river (Kanchanaburi is a popular local holiday spot) before the majesty of the river, banked by rain forest and hundreds of lotus ponds, and surrounded by distant hazy green mountains, imposes itself. Later, we disembark at a small dock and make our way through a forest clearing to the impeccably maintained Chung Kai War Cemetery, one of three war cemeteries in the area. Here lie the remains of some 1,740 mainly British and Dutch soldiers, brought down by disease, starvation, exhaustion, and execution during the building of the railway. Passengers slowly wander around the perfectly manicured lawns sprinkled with pink and white frangipani flowers, reading names and poetic epitaphs on the simple, uniform gravestones. On the gravestone of A.R.R. Robson, of the Royal Northumberland Fusiliers, who died on November 9, 1943, at age 24, his parents have left this epitaph: "A smiling face, a heart of gold, to us his dear memory will never grow old."

Not much later, but six hours behind schedule, the *Eastern & Oriental Express* is rolling into Bangkok's Hua Lamphong Railway Station. It's 8:30 p.m. The graciousness and ease of pace encountered over the last 47 hours is quickly swallowed up by this steamy, chaotic capital city and is replaced by din, traffic, and pollution. I gather my bag from the platform, hop in a taxi, and head toward the Oriental, a hotel that edges the banks of the Chao Phraya River, the capital's main waterway. The Oriental has been around for more than a century and a quarter and it is the grandest of all Asia's colonial hotels. The original building houses the Authors' Residence, sumptuous suites whose rooms carry names of famous authors who have slept there: Joseph Conrad, Noël Coward, and Somerset Maugham. I'm led to the James Michener suite, with its 15-foot-high ceilings, a magnificent claw-foot bath the size of a small swimming pool, and views of the river and hotel gardens.

I make my way down to the riverfront, sit on the hotel's terrace, and watch the river traffic speed by. A breeze kicks up from the river, cooling the sweltering evening air.

Tug boats haul huge teak barges toward the city's port of Khlong Toie. Sleek longtail boats with threatening engines mounted on their sterns zoom past at breakneck speed with passengers hanging on to the gunwales, and small, jaunty river taxis bob up and down at the river's edge waiting for fares. I turn the pages of a Southeast Asian travel guide I had taken on my journey and reread for about the 30th time a quote the remarkable Victorian adventurer Isabella Bird had bequeathed to Southeast Asia:

Oh that you could see it all! It is wonderful; no words could describe it, far less mine. Mr. Darwin says so truly that a visit to the tropics (and such tropics) is like a visit to a new planet. This new wonder-world, so enchanting, tantalising, intoxicating, makes me despair, for I cannot make you see what I am seeing!

THE INDIAN PACIFIC

By Roff Smith

Photos by
Kerry Trapnell

An air of expectancy hung over platforms two and three at Sydney's Central Railway Station,

where the two halves of the *Indian Pacific* were being prepared for its journey. At more than 1,600 feet long, its silvery cavalcade of sleepers, diners, day carriages, and baggage vans was too long for any single platform. I walked beside it, ticket in one hand, overnight bag in the other, looking for Car H and savoring that thrill of imminent departure that you can only ever feel on a railway platform. Porters bustled, suitcases were hauled on board, and families and couples hugged, kissed, and snapped pictures of each other. The big silver sleeper cars, aloof and cool and private with their blinds intriguingly half closed, the windows of the diners, where little sprigs of flowers adorned each table, projected jazzy sophistication.

Other trains make a call on stylishness and glamour, too, and nostalgia for travel the way it used to be. But what makes the *Indian Pacific* special is the fact that after it leaves Sydney and its glorious sail-filled harbor, it heads straight out into some of the world's harshest, loneliest, and most forbidding terrain as it makes an epic 2,702-mile transcontinental run to Perth. Only the *Trans-Siberian* is a longer ride. And with the exception of a pause in genteel Adelaide, about a thousand miles west of Sydney, virtually the entire journey is in the outback, across endless expanses of saltbush, eucalyptus scrub, and vast arid plains.

Over the next three days and nights this sleek train will stop, refuel, and take on water and passengers at dusty mining towns. Long mournful blasts from its horn will send mobs of kangaroos and emus bounding away from tracks. At the end of the line, on the far side of the desolate Nullarbor Plain, rises the gleaming, tinted-glass skyline of Perth, said to be the world's

PRECEDING PAGES: *An abandoned car provides some visual relief from emptiness around the outback ghost town of Cook. While employed by the railway, Bruce Hutchison and his family (and their 17 dogs) were the town's sole residents, relying on the Indian Pacific to bring supplies.*

most isolated big city, sitting alone on the rim of the Indian Ocean, closer to the Indonesian capital of Jakarta than to Sydney.

Farther along the platform men in bright plastic safety vests finished loading cars on the motor-rail carriages. Some of them were crammed with belongings—the boxes, quilts, suitcases, and valuables of people who

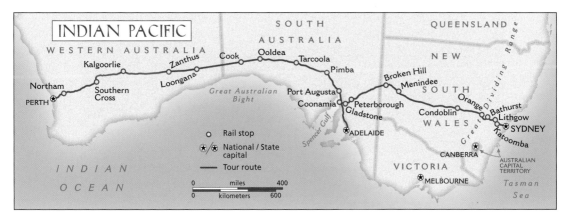

had packed up and were heading west, lock, stock, and barrel, to start a new life. It made me think of the old *20th Century Limited* meeting the Oregon Trail.

I found Car H. An attendant, authoritative in dark blue livery, yet who introduced himself with breezy Australian insouciance as "Johno," tore a page off my ticket and showed me to my cabin. It was cozy, in dark wood and brass fittings and upholstered in earth tones. The upper corner of the dresser mirror was elegantly frosted in Aboriginal pointillist motifs, which flowed around an etching of a wedge-tailed eagle, a magnificent outback bird of prey that is also the logo of the *Indian Pacific*. Another wedge-tailed eagle adorned the cover of the train's timetable, a copy of which waited on my seat. I picked it up and flipped through it. There were 86 crossing loops, or sidings, along the line. Most were obscure settlements or desert ghost towns—places such as Wirraminna, Ooldea, and Zanthus—that the train would rumble straight through. Most are not designated stopping points, but stops may be made by prearrangement. I tried to imagine climbing off the train at, say, Wirraminna at 3:02 a.m., two nights from now, which is when the timetable said we'd pass through.

A slight jolt told me they were putting the train together. A few minutes later I noticed a bench and a knot of people waving farewell slide furtively past my window. We were moving. I glanced at my watch. Five minutes to three: dead on time.

The train gathered pace slowly, almost imperceptibly. Gritty brick platforms of Sydney's inner-city stations glided by: Redfern, Newtown, Petersham. I finished my coffee and began settling in: unpacking clothes, hanging my coat and shirts in the cupboard, and setting out my toilet kit in the bathroom. This Pullman-size compartment was going to be my home for the next few days. Such unbuttoned easiness was a luxury early travelers didn't have.

Sure, there were sleepers and saloon cars and diners, complete with white-jacketed stewards and silver cutlery, even on Australia's first transcontinental rail journey in October 1917—but there was no settling in for the duration. Perth-bound passengers had to change trains several times en route.

The reason goes back to grand old 19th-century British Empire days, when mainland Australia was a clutch of bickering colonies—New South Wales, Victoria, South Australia, Queensland, and Western Australia—whose leaders could not agree on anything, let alone a standard railway gauge. The engineers of Victoria's railroads were Irishmen—so they patriotically chose the wide Irish gauge. New South Wales opted for standard British gauge. Western Australians economized with narrow gauge. And so it went. The result was chaos, something out of the pages of Evelyn Waugh.

Although the colonies put aside their differences in 1901 and united to

Sydney's Central Railway Station—a cavernous 1906 sandstone building in the heart of the city—is both a commuter hub and the springboard for the 65-hour odyssey to Perth.

form the nation we know today as Australia, the tangled legacy of the colonial railroads endured for decades. A traveler who wanted to go from Sydney to Perth had to take the ironically named *Spirit of Progress* to Albury-Wodonga, on the Victorian border, and then change to another train bound for the dusty South Australian lead-smelting town of Port Pirie. There he could board the *Trans-Australian Express*—better known as "The Trans"—for the 1,400-mile trek across the desert to Perth. It wasn't until 1970 that it was possible to ride the same train all the way. That was the year the *Indian Pacific* was born.

WE HUMMED ALONG THROUGH SYDNEY'S SPRAWLING WEST, PASSING RATTLING commuter trains and whisking through a string of dreary suburban platforms at a gratifying speed. But the breath of the bush is never very far away, even in Australia's biggest cities. Within an hour the suburbs had thinned out and the *Indian Pacific* had started the long grade into the Blue Mountains, an ancient wilderness about 3,000 feet high that runs along the east coast.

I threaded my way down to the lounge car, bought a bottle of Tasmanian beer, and watched the forests close in around us. The Blue Mountains get their name from the haze of eucalyptus oil given off by these forests. It makes them appear smudgy and blue, like an old oil painting, from a distance. Although not high, they are so steep and wild and formidable that it took Australia's early settlers 25 years to find a way through them.

It was easy to see why, as the train snaked its way up one in thirty-three grades, bored through tunnels, and rounded exposed curves, where miles of blue-green wilderness spilled away beneath us. This was Australia's great divide. Beyond these mountains was a broad dusty outback, more than two million square miles of desert, plains, and scrub, stretching to the Indian Ocean. My ears popped. An excited woman claimed the first kangaroo sighting of the journey. We hadn't yet gone 70 miles—of the 2,702 in front of us—and already the city seemed a distant memory. But not civilization: The stylish lounge car buzzed with chatter, the clink of glasses, laughter. I found myself talking cattle with Don and Marie Wright, graziers who had run a 4,000-acre cattle property in the rich grasslands near Tamworth, about 200 miles north of Sydney. "This has been one of the best ever years for cattle, but after 48 years we decided it was time to pass it on to our son and move into town," Marie explained. "Then take a bit of time out and see the country."

Over by the bar, a couple of hearty-voiced men talked Australian rules footy: Essendon's chances of another premiership, Sydney's hopes for a spot in the finals. A retired coal miner and his wife from the Hunter Valley

Restaurant worker Raisa Yudasin takes a break as the afternoon shadows lengthen over Sydney's iconic Harbour Bridge. Australians may love their sunburnt country, but the vast majority choose to live and work near the sea. More than one in five live in Sydney.

FOLLOWING PAGES: *Sparkling like a jewel on the rim of the South Pacific, Sydney is one of the world's most cosmopolitan cities. But the breath of the bush is never far away—and neither are its dangers, with bushfires occasionally sweeping into the suburbs.*

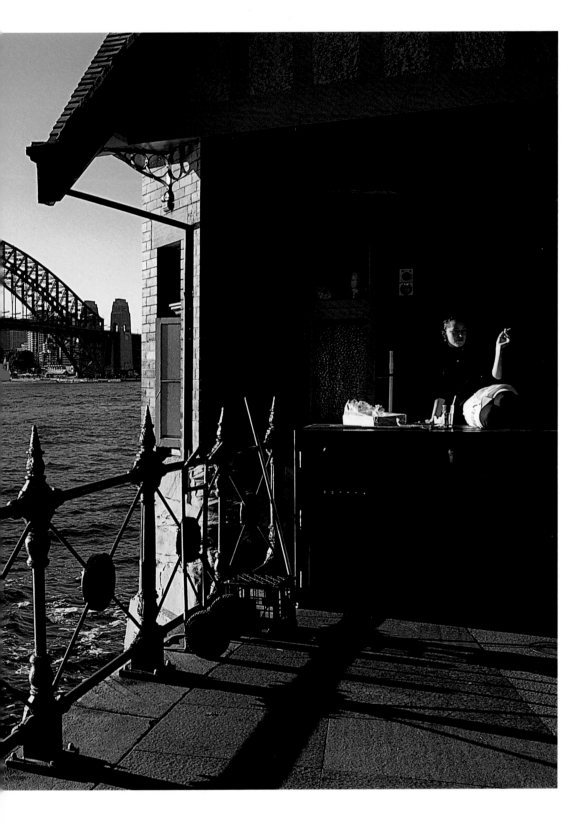

reminisced with an old country doctor and his wife, from down in Victoria. From a few seats away came more voices: "No, no, mate, it's my shout," one bloke argued amiably with another, getting up to buy the next round of beers. I smiled. For all the gracious Pullman-style ambience, what we had here was a good old Aussie pub, rolling slowly into the outback.

As in any country pub, spontaneous mateship can spring up over a couple of beers between strangers. "We had a couple of old gents traveling to Perth recently," train manager Michael Pantich recalled with a smile. "They were both over 70 and they hit it right off. After a few beers they went to dinner together. One of the guys really fancied a steak. But when he sat down at the table he realized that he'd left his false teeth back in Sydney. 'No worries, mate!' cried his new friend. 'I've got a spare pair back in me cabin!' "

SHADOWS LENGTHENED INTO NIGHT. WE SNAKED IN DARKNESS THROUGH THE mountains. The dining car was brightly lit and cheerful. I ordered a Caesar salad and fillet of kangaroo, done in an Illawarra plum glaze with a sprig of native pepper leaf for garnish. An excellent Shiraz from South Australia's Coonawarra region rounded it off. This was the outback with style. I had a nightcap in the lounge car as we rolled through the coal-mining country around Lithgow, and retired with a copy of Ernestine Hill's 1937 travel classic *The Great Australian Loneliness*. An inveterate traveler and correspondent for the *Sydney Morning Herald*, Hill wandered the outback on her own for five years—traveling by packhorse, biplane, coastal steamer, and rail—during the Great Depression years. I read propped up in my bunk. Her stories, of Afghan cameleers and pearling luggers and gruff men who hunted water buffalo for a living, belonged to a Joseph Conrad world I would have thought had vanished more than a century ago. But this was everyday life in the Australian outback just 20 years before I was born. The gentle swaying of the train rocked me to sleep.

I woke before dawn and looked out the window. A faint glow, from the night manager's berth perhaps, at the end of the carriage, illuminated the weeds along the track. They flickered past, ghostly pale. We were moving right along. The night was velvety blue. There were no lights from towns or houses, but the stars were blazing. The Southern Cross hung low on the horizon. I had camped enough in the bush to know by the way the cross was tilted that sunrise was at least another hour away. I was too restless to go back to sleep. Like a kid, I plumped up my pillow, watched and waited, and marveled at the vast and empty landscape that eventually materialized in the gray morning light. This was the magic of the night train: While we'd

Little more than an hour out of the city, but already a world away, the
Indian Pacific *lumbers through dense bush in the Blue Mountains.*
West of this range lie more than 2,000 miles of dusty wide-open
outback—all the way to Perth, on the far side of the continent.

Famed as the Silver City, Broken Hill has prospered for nearly 120 years on the back of a single boomerang-shaped mother lode four miles long, and the richest of its kind ever found. More recently its clear desert light and outback location has made it a popular setting with film directors.

PRECEDING PAGES: *Sunrise brings a glimpse of the Menindee Lakes, a sprawling oasis for waterbirds on the arid plains of western New South Wales. The lakes, which are larger than Sydney Harbour, supply water for the outback mining town of Broken Hill.*

*"I shall return." In the darkest days of World War II, retreating
U.S. Gen. Douglas MacArthur reiterated his grim promise to
recapture the Philippines in a short speech on the platform of
South Australia's Terowie railway station, where he broke his rail
journey south from Alice Springs.*

slept the *Indian Pacific* had slid down the western flank of the ranges, sped across New South Wales's broad pastoral districts, and was now rattling across the desolate arid plains, true outback, more than 600 miles from Sydney. We could have ridden back through the pages of the book I had been reading, now sprawled open on the cabin floor—nothing out here would have changed much since Ernestine Hill's time.

There was no shortage of wildlife. Daybreak revealed scores of kangaroos and emus, standing idly beside the tracks as though they had just been spilled out of the ark and were wondering what to do next. A series of long wailing blasts from the locomotive's horn sent them scattering into the bush. The low, raking honey-colored sunlight that lit the scene gave texture and depth to the miles of dead flat saltbush and highlighted the brassy flanks of the kangaroos as they bounded away. They were western reds, the kings of the outback, growing up to six feet tall and weighing in at up to 200 pounds. There were so many of them. It was magnificent: the incarnation of the most theatrically shot Australian wildlife documentary you could hope for. And as one scene swept past the window, another, equally stirring, slipped into its place.

We pulled into Broken Hill at a quarter to eight, local time. The dusty silver-mining town is so far removed from anyplace else in New South Wales that the locals use South Australian time, meaning we had to set our watches back half an hour. The place was dead quiet. It was too early for the pubs to be open, even here. The train changed crews here at Broken Hill and took on fuel and water, so there was time to step out and look around.

It was cool and crisp. A soft breeze carried the spicy tang of the Australian bush. Passengers shuffled along the platform, stretching, blinking, exchanging good mornings, and scratching their heads at the enormous mountain of slag that dominated the south side of the town: a legacy of more than a century of boom-time mining. I set off for a stroll along Argent Street, the town's main drag, while most passengers took the organized tour. A crow cawed lazily.

It felt like a movie set. Broken Hill's streetscape of iron-roofed miners' cottages, its Italianate town hall, and the cavalcade of two- and three-story Victorian pubs along Argent Street, their deep shady verandas trimmed with cast-iron lace, seems to rise out of nowhere on a saltbush sea. Indeed, if it weren't for fabulously rich deposits of silver, lead, and zinc, none of this would be here. A boundary rider named Charles Rasp discovered the lode in 1883, while riding the plains with a "How to Prospect" guide tucked in his saddlebag. A brawling city of 30,000 sprang up almost overnight, miles from anywhere and almost totally without water. Broken Hill has lived on this lucky strike ever since. But even on the town's main drag you can't escape the sense of isolation. I glanced at my watch. The hour had sped by quickly. I picked up my pace.

Back at the station attendants were ushering people aboard the train. Within minutes we were away, rolling across a dusty immensity of earth and sky, with kangaroos and emus spurting out of the bush. Broken Hill—one of Australia's biggest outback towns—had vanished as abruptly as a mirage.

I settled into my cabin, put my feet up, and read a little, while the sun arched higher. Lunchtime came and went, with almost a shipboard somnolence. The tracks made a long slow bend to the south, past the lower end of the Flinders Ranges and through the hardscrabble wheat country of what South Australians quixotically call "the mid-north." When I glanced up, mid-afternoon, the countryside had softened. It was green with winter rains and dotted with farmhouses. The houses grew closer together; there were suburbs and shopping malls, and then we were in Adelaide.

THE LEAFY SOUTH AUSTRALIAN CAPITAL—THE MOST GENTEEL OF AUSTRALIA'S capital cities and known as the City of Churches—is the only city along the whole 2,702-mile length of the *Indian Pacific*'s run, and our last glimpse of civilization before heading out across the vast Nullarbor Plain. This is where the outback adventure really begins. The train laid up here for two and a half hours, changing crews, refueling, taking on water and food, making whatever minor repairs needed to be done, and adding a few more carriages. It was nearly half a mile long when it pulled out of town at half past six. "We have to be pretty self-sufficient out there," explained Doug Payne, a third-generation railroad man and a porter for 33 years, as he showed me around the well-stocked workshop car near the rear of the train. "This train is basically a small town on wheels."

It needs to be. Five hours from now, just before midnight, when the *Indian Pacific* rumbles out of the outback town of Port Augusta, we will be heading into the heart of a desert so vast and empty that we will not see another town until we reach the West Australian goldfields, more than a thousand miles later—unless, of course, you care to count the ghost-town sidings of Cook (population 4) or Forrest (population 2). Nothing but two ribbons of steel stretch from treeless horizon to treeless horizon. The eerily lonely Eyre Highway, which is the only other overland route to Perth, hugs the cliffs along the coast more than 60 miles to the south. Once out on the Nullarbor, *Indian Pacific* is as on its own as the old wagon trains crossing the prairie.

To anyone living in North America or Europe, such isolation is hard to comprehend. As late as the 1960s the "highway" to Perth was a brutal

*Locomotive drivers Peter Zemetis (left)
and Patrick Whittaker (right) cruise at a
stately 70 miles an hour across the
Nullarbor Plain, frequently blowing
the horn to scatter the kangaroos that
gather to nibble the wild hops sprouting
along the tracks.*

FOLLOWING PAGES: *A sign along the
desolate stretch of track just outside the
South Australian town of Cook tells
passengers they have traveled 912
kilometers from Coonamia. On the
featureless desert the progression of these
little posts can sometimes seem like the
only tangible evidence of motion.*

For 12 hours the Indian Pacific *rolls across Australia's famous treeless, waterless void. Covering more than 100,000 square miles, the Nullarbor Plain was once an ancient seabed, until it rose out of the water about ten million years ago.*

sandy track, 1,500 miles long, and any easterner who drove a car across it was likely to get his story in the local paper. It wasn't much easier by air. Up until the 1990s, when wide-bodied Boeing 767s took over the route, "nonstop" cross-country flights to Perth often stopped in Adelaide anyway to take on more fuel before attempting to fly over these vast and windy wastes. The two people who reside in Forrest are caretakers for an airstrip—capable of handling a big jet—still kept in readiness for emergency desert landings, because there is nothing out there if a plane gets into trouble.

Or if a person does. "We had a passenger once who became very seriously ill when we were out on the Nullarbor," Doug Payne told me. "We radioed the Royal Flying Doctor Service," he said, referring to Australia's legendary outback medical service that provides free treatment and air evacuation to anyone stricken in the bush. "Fortunately we were just coming up on Forrest when we called them, and their plane was coming in as we arrived. Perfect timing. They whisked her away to the hospital in Kalgoorlie."

Although the *Indian Pacific* isn't the lifeline to Perth that it once was—most of its passengers now travel overland for the experience, not out of necessity—it's still the way west for a small but steady tide of adventurers, drifters, and outcasts.

"I'm on a mission," a hard-voiced woman named Mary Ann told me, as she shook loose a cigarette from a crumpled pack and fished around in her knapsack for a lighter. She was in her mid-30s, for a guess, but she looked older. She wore a tattered army-surplus sweater, a watchful smile, and had the words L-O-V-E and H-A-T-E tattooed on the knuckles of her hands. She looked as tough as Grendel's aunt.

We were talking in the rear of the train, where a couple of carriages of upright day/night seats offered cheap passage across the continent to anybody willing and able to sit up for three days and nights. It was crowded. An unwatched video played noisily overhead. Somebody was snoring. I leaned against the doorway, balancing against the swaying motion of the train. "What's the mission?"

"I'm going to break up with my boyfriend." There was fierce joy in her voice. "I'm coming across the continent—3,000 miles—just for this. Face to face."

"Is it worth it?"

"Oh yeah." Her smile became reptilian. "It's worth it. It is to me. I love confrontation. I just love it. Back in Broken Hill I picked up a couple of bloody big rocks to bash him with in case he wants to get violent. I'm ready for anything, I don't care."

"Well that sounds—uh—gee, does he know you're coming?"

"Nope."

A vision came to me of a front door opening somewhere in Perth two mornings from now and Mary Ann standing there, arms wide in greeting and a rock in each hand. Hell coming to breakfast. "Guess he'll be surprised to see you then."

She gave a throaty laugh. "Yeah, I'm kind of looking forward to see-

ing his face. Stick around in Perth a few days. If you see a story in the paper about a woman from Sydney murdering her ex-boyfriend, you'll know it's me." She shrugged, then laughed again. "Then again, maybe nothing much will happen. Who knows? Anyway, after I've sorted him out I figure I'll head up to the Kimberley. Start over. I've always wanted to go up there. You been?"

"It's nice."

She had been rolling the unlit cigarette around in her fingers for some time now, casting fidgety glances to the smoking area at the rear of the car. "Will you excuse me?" She balanced her way down the aisle, waving a greeting to a heavy-boned man named Walt, a fellow smoker, who had just left his job at a meatpacking plant in Victoria and was drifting west to check out prospects there. They shared a match. I stayed leaning against the doorway,

As night falls over the desert, passengers gather for a quiet beer in
Hannan's Lounge, a bar car named in honor of Paddy Hannan, the
Irish prospector who sparked one of the world's biggest gold rushes
when he found nuggets near present-day Kalgoorlie in 1893.

For truck driver Mick Hunter the westbound Indian Pacific *is the ticket to a new life in Perth, Western Australia's gleaming capital city on the other side of "the paddock," as Australia's truckers usually refer to the Nullarbor Plain.*

OPPOSITE: *The train stops briefly for a crew change at the lonely outpost of Cook, giving passengers an opportunity to get out and stretch their legs. Train managers Greg Fisher and David Littledike make sure everyone is back on board before the train pulls out.*

PRECEDING PAGES: *Known as the Super Pit, the huge open-cut gold mine on the outskirts of Kalgoorlie produces more than 800,000 troy ounces of gold each year, with no end in sight.*

thinking this train was as full of stories as a boarding house, and looking out at the lights of a distant farm as we sped through the South Australian night.

⋙◆⋘

MORNING BROKE COOL AND GRAY. WE'D LEFT BEHIND THE LEAN-RIBBED FARMLANDS of the mid-north, and were rolling now across a desert of low, red dunes and thick scrub. A few stray droplets of rain streaked the windows, and the sullen skies made everything dreary and flat. I dawdled over eggs and coffee in the dining car, nodding to the now familiar faces on our second morning out, as miles of outback desert slid past the window like the reel of a closed-circuit film. Only the progression of abandoned railway sidings—marked by weather-beaten signs saying Wynbring, Mungala, or Bates—every 40 miles or so gave proof that this wasn't just some endless tape, that we were in fact moving west.

"It's a big country, isn't it?" cattleman Don Wright remarked, as he looked out the dining car window. That phrase had become kind of a mantra among the *Indian Pacific*'s travelers by now, murmured periodically, often with a slow disbelieving shake of the head, as the everlasting outback rolled by. Australia is indeed a big country—about as large as the continental United States, but with the exception of the fertile crescent along its east coast, mostly uninhabitable. This was the Great Victorian Desert we were seeing now, and it stretched for hundreds of miles into the interior of the continent, where it melded imperceptibly with the Simpson Desert to the northeast and the Gibson and Great Sandy Deserts to the northwest. It is experiencing this vastness—the Great Australian Loneliness—that is the *Indian Pacific*'s almost mythical appeal; and why crossing the continent overland is virtually an Australian right of passage. "There is nothing out here," laughs Doug Payne. "But it is the finest nothing in the world."

And we hadn't even hit the Nullarbor Plain. That came a little after breakfast, and as open and wide as the Great Victorian Desert had seemed, spilling onto the Nullarbor was like coming out of a tunnel. Gnarled eucalyptuses and the rolling dunes suddenly fell away, to be replaced by—absolutely nothing. The land was dead flat and utterly empty of all but ankle-high scrub as far as the eye could see—and indeed much, much farther than that. More than 400 miles of hard-baked limestone would pass under our wheels before we would see another tree. Cups of tea grew cold, conversations petered out, and books lay forgotten as all of us stared out the window and tried to comprehend such scale and emptiness.

It was given its name in 1865 by South Australian surveyor Edmund Delisser, from the Latin for "no tree"—*nullus arbor*. It is a chunk of ancient seabed that rose out of the ocean about ten million years ago. Delisser could just as accurately have named the Nullarbor "No Water," because there are no life-sustaining pools or creeks anywhere on this hundred-thousand-square-mile void. Less than ten inches of rain falls each year, while the bone-dry air sucks much more than that out of the meager soil. Tem-

peratures routinely soar above 120 degrees in the summer and drop below freezing on bitter winter nights. Harsh winds blow constantly. The Aborigines rarely ventured far into it.

For the early white explorers, it was a nightmare of thirst and heat and flies and maddeningly receding horizons. "A hideous anomaly, a blot on the face of Nature, the sort of place one gets into in bad dreams," wrote a jittery Edward John Eyre, who barely survived the first known crossing of the plain in 1841. A later explorer expressed himself in more earthy terms: "Any man who would travel this country for pleasure would go to hell for a pastime."

They started building the railway across the Nullarbor in 1913. It was an enormous undertaking—costing about $500 million in today's terms, and involving 150,000 tons of 80-pound rail and more than 2.5 million sleepers

Friday night draws customers to the pub in Broad Arrow, one of the fading gold rush towns in the Western Australian goldfields. The lure of gold nuggets still brings independent prospectors to seek their fortunes. In 1990 one lucky digger found a nugget containing 97 ounces of gold.

A surfer at Perth's popular Cottesloe Beach
washes off the salt water after a day spent
riding the Indian Ocean's glassy rollers.

An old pavilion graces Cottesloe Beach, where much of Perth spends
its sunny weekends. After a three-day journey across the world's
driest inhabited continent, a short taxi ride brings you to the end of
the line: the salty blue horizon of the Indian Ocean. The next landfall
from here is Africa.

cut out of tough, heavy termite-resistant jarrah wood. Since there was noth-ing out on the Nullarbor Plain to support the work camps—no food or water, no shelter, no trees to cut for fuel—everything had to be specially hauled out there, often by camels, on ever longer supply lines as the tracks stretched deeper into the desert. After the line opened in 1917, one-third of all cargo carried by the trains was simply water and coal for the 52 remote supply depots and repair camps along the line.

"With the building of the railway, a chain of tiny settlements has sprung up in the desolation, a unique community of railway fettlers and gangers constantly working to keep the line from creeping and crippling in the heat," wrote Ernestine Hill. "...Cook, in the centre of them, has become a street of big comfortable bungalows in the very heart of Nullarbor, with...a school, a church, a cemetery, a slaughter-yard, a locomotive workshop and a store. The 'Trans' and its people are a little world sufficient for themselves."

It was a curiously lonely little world that lasted up until the mid-1980s. Every week a supply train—known to locals as the Tea and Sugar—ran out from Port Augusta, stopping off at each of these isolated little settlements on the Nullarbor.

"The Tea and Sugar had everything, it was like a rolling main street," Doug Payne told me over a cup of coffee during his break. He had worked the famous old supply train for years. "There was a nice little grocery store set up in one carriage, a post office, a bank and pay office, a butcher shop, dry goods, tank cars filled with water, everything. The best run was around Christmastime when one of the men would play Santa Claus and visit the kids at the sidings."

But when the old wooden sleepers were replaced by modern concrete ones, which require almost no maintenance, there was no longer any need for work crews to live along the tracks. "A whole way of life just vanished," Payne said sadly. The little siding towns were soon abandoned—except for Cook, once known as the Queen City of the Nullarbor. But it too is virtually a ghost town, its bungalows empty and forlorn. Only four people were liv-ing there: Bruce and Michelle Hutchison and their two small children, Brody and Jackson. They looked after the relief crews and saw to the refueling of the *Indian Pacific* on its twice-weekly run.

We pulled in a little after ten o'clock. It was cool and breezy. A three-legged dog trotted along Cook's single dusty street, amiably scrounging pats and tidbits from the passengers as they spread out from the train, looking dazedly at the emptiness stretching to every horizon. A couple of young guys in their early 20s stretched their legs by kicking a football around in the dust. Most of the rest of the passengers shuffled over to the old school building to buy cups of coffee or ice creams or souvenir postcards from the Hutchisons. The murmured conversations, the thud of the football in the dust, seemed to magnify the immense hush that settled over this flat and empty world.

"There sure is a lot of freedom out here," Bruce said, reaching down to pat the dog. Behind him, nailed on a wall, a rough hand-painted sign taken from one of the abandoned rabbit shooters' camps warned: "Any arsehole that steals from this camp will be gut shot and left for the eagles to feed on." He noticed that I was staring at it and smiled. "Oh yeah, him. He didn't get on very well with his neighbors. He's gone now, but he's been talking about coming back."

"Do you reckon that sign is serious?"

He shrugged. "Anything could happen out there—and who'd know? You wouldn't think to look at it now, but just a few years ago these little siding towns were real Wild West sorts of places."

I had an idea I might just believe it.

<hr />

COOK IS PERCHED ALONGSIDE THE WORLD'S LONGEST STRETCH OF DEAD STRAIGHT track—298 miles. Up in the cab of the locomotive it looks like two shimmering parallel lines stretching out to meet at infinity, with clumps of glorious red wildflowers sprouting from the sides of the tracks and a drab expanse of earth and sky everywhere else.

"It is like sailing on an ocean of grass," locomotive driver Johnny Ray laughed, tapping the "dead man's button." It's easy to become hypnotized by hours of such rhythmic monotony, so drivers work in two-man crews, and computers require them to do something to indicate they are awake and alert. "Unless one of us hits this button every 90 seconds," he explained, "blue lights start flashing on the console, then a piercing siren sounds and, if it still isn't pushed at that point, the emergency brakes come on and stop the train."

A native New Zealander, Ray has been working Australia's outback railroads for 38 years, much of that time driving the two-mile-long iron-ore trains in the rugged northwest, hauling thousands of tons of ore from a remote mine deep in the desert to the loading docks at Karratha, a lonely port sweltering on the Indian Ocean. "Those are some of the heaviest trains in the world—more than 20,000 gross tons," he said. "The Indian Pacific is a nice trim 1,485 tons. After so many years of crawling along with a load of iron ore it's kind of nice to be moving at a decent speed."

I wondered what he meant, because it looked to me as though we were barely moving, just idling our way along the tracks. And then I glanced at the speedometer. We were traveling at more than 70 miles an hour. I would have sworn I could have stepped off and walked.

Later, back in the lounge car, I thought about Ray's description of sailing on a sea of grass. A crossing on the *Indian Pacific* did feel more like a sea voyage than a rail journey: Like a ship on a quiet sea, the train became our own little world, and the few towns we saw like little ports of call; our days passed in genteel idleness and a cozy routine of breakfast, lunch, and dinner in the diner, with the familiar faces of fellow travelers. All we needed

was shuffleboard. As the sun arched overhead and into another afternoon, we read, we ate, we rested, and hurtled across the Nullarbor—I was still stunned that we were doing more than 70 miles an hour—absorbing more of the sublime grandeur of the outback.

The sun was setting when the first few trees came into view on the western fringes of the Nullarbor. After so many hours "out there," seeing these scrubby eucalyptus trees was like a return to civilization, although we were still nearly four hours from the desert town of Kalgoorlie—and from there it was another 406 mostly empty miles to the skyline of Perth. But the trees meant the Nullarbor was behind us, we had crossed the forbidding

A bush motif of kangaroos, koalas, and kookaburras adorns the cardholder passenger Pat Halls devised for herself and her elderly card-playing friends, many of whom have arthritis.

FOLLOWING PAGES: *A stand of eucalyptus trees near the old siding town of Zanthus, on the western edge of the Nullarbor Plain, slides by the window of the* Indian Pacific.

physical and mental barrier that divides Australia; we were in the west now.

It was dark when we rolled into Kalgoorlie, a rollicking gold-mining town of 27,000 squatting on one of the world's richest square miles of land. A prospector named Paddy Hannan discovered nuggets beneath a tree out here in 1893, and a century later the rush is still on. Amateur prospectors still find whopping nuggets—some barely buried under the soil. More than 800,000 troy ounces of gold each year come out of the "Super Pit," a huge open-cut mine on the edge of town.

We paused here for another change of drivers. I took a leg stretcher along Hannan Street, Kalgoorlie's main drag. It was Saturday night—a time of darkened sidewalks, squealing rubber, and throaty muscle cars roaring up the street, jukebox sounds and hard brassy laughter spilling out of crowded pubs, and the gleam of slot machines through the gaming-room windows. A lot of fat paychecks from the mines were being burned up tonight. It was only a little after eight o'clock. Kalgoorlie wouldn't really be hitting its stride for another couple of hours.

But by then I was in bed and we were miles away, rolling through the darkness toward Perth and the Indian Ocean. I slept well—and late. I woke to diffuse sunlight spilling in through the window. I blinked, piecing together the irritating fact that I must have forgotten to draw the blinds. I sat up and looked out. We were rolling through the Avon Valley, where the sun was burning through a morning mist. The hills were green and steep, and the floodplain was dotted with large, handsome gum trees. The river splashed between rocks and swirled in wide brown pools. It seemed almost parklike, especially after the numbing sterility of the Nullarbor Plain. There were houses and fences and roads. Horses and cattle nibbled the grass. They passed in a blur. I showered and packed and had breakfast for the last time with the familiar faces in the dining car.

We rattled through level crossings, red lights flashing and the barriers down, a clutch of cars held up as the *Indian Pacific* whisked by in a silvery whoosh. It felt as though the train could smell the sea after the hundreds of miles of desert and knew it was on the home stretch. At Midlands we broke stride long enough to pick up a quarantine officer, who ambled along the swaying corridors asking passengers if they had any fresh fruit, honey, or raw nuts. It was like coming into a foreign port. The deserts we had passed through isolate Perth as effectively as any ocean. Fifteen minutes later we drew into the station. It was a sparkling Sunday morning, the glass-and-steel skyline taut against a bold sky. I took a room at a hotel, and wanting to finish what I had started, hailed a cab to take me the final 12 miles to the port of Fremantle, where the waters of the Indian Ocean lapped the western edge of Australia.

ABOUT THE CONTRIBUTORS

CHRIS ANDERSON is currently a contract photographer for *US News & World Report* and a regular contributor to *The New York Times Magazine* and *National Geographic Adventure*. Honors for his work include the Robert Capa Gold Medal for pictures of an attempt by Haitian immigrants to sail to America, the Visa d'Or in Perpignan, France, for his work on the Afghan refugee crisis, the Kodak Young Photographer of the Year Award for his story about the Stone Throwers of Gaza, and various Pictures of the Year awards. He is a member of the prestigious agency VII.

Born in British Columbia, Canada, in 1970, Chris spent much of his life in Texas and Colorado before moving to New York City and eventually to Paris, where he currently lives.

Exhibitions include Visa Pour L'Image in Perpignan, France, and the Gallerie Dupon in Paris.

RON FISHER has contributed to National Geographic publications for many years—first as a staff writer and editor with Special Publications and in the Book Division and since retiring in 1994, as a freelancer. A native of Iowa, he now lives in Arlington, Virginia.

DOUGLAS BENNETT LEE is a freelance writer and filmmaker who has lived intermittently in Africa since 1988, when National Geographic sent him on assignment to Botswana's Okavango Delta. He grew up in an expatriate oil-business family, in Manila, Tokyo, Kuwait, and London, before returning to the United States for university, and then working for 15 years as a staff writer and editor for NATIONAL GEOGRAPHIC magazine.

PHIL MACDONALD left his native Australia in 1989 to work as a journalist in Hong Kong. He now lives in Bangkok, Thailand, working as a freelance journalist and editor, contributing to regional and international publications. He is co-author of *National Geographic Traveler: Thailand* and author of *National Geographic Traveler: Hong Kong*.

PHIL SCHERMEISTER As a freelance photographer for the National Geographic Society and other clients since 1985, Phil Schermeister has crisscrossed North America working on such projects as the Tarahumara Indians of Mexico, the Pony Express Trail, and the Cherokee Indian Trail of Tears. Based in California, he has a wide variety of editorial and corporate clients and concentrates much of his editorial work on environmental issues in California and nationwide.

While a student at the University of Minnesota School of Journalism, Schermeister was selected as the College Photographer of the Year by the National Press Photographers Association. After graduation, he headed to Kansas to work as a newspaper photographer for six years before starting work as a freelancer.

He has recently completed several books for National Geographic's Book Division including *Range of Light: The Sierra Nevada Mountains* and *Guide to Outdoor America: Far West*.

He and his wife, Laureen, and their two daughters live in the Sierra Nevada foothills town of Sonora, California.

ROFF SMITH Australian writer Roff Smith has traveled widely during his 15-year career in journalism. In 1997 he made a 10,000-mile journey by bicycle through the Australian outback. He lives near Adelaide, in South Australia, where he writes for a number of international magazines and publications, including the National Geographic Society.

TINO SORIANO Born in Barcelona, Spain, Tino Soriano shares his work as a photojournalist with travel photography. He has received a First Prize from World Press Photo Foundation and awards from UNESCO, WHO, MILK, Fujifilm Photographer of the Year, and FOTOPRES—the most important Spanish award for press photography—among others. His reportage has been projected and exhibited in the Festival International de Photojournalism Visa Pour L'image. He has been a contributor to National Geographic since 1998.

SCOTT THYBONY has written books for the National Geographic Society on the Rocky Mountains and the American Southwest, and has worked as a contributing editor for *National Geographic Traveler*. His work has appeared in NATIONAL GEOGRAPHIC magazine, and the National Geographic Expeditions Council awarded him one of its first exploration grants. Having lived with a Navajo medicine man in Arizona and an Inuit family in the Arctic, he brings to his writing an enthusiasm for the natural world and those who live close to it.

KERRY TRAPNELL is an Australian who lives in Cairns, North Queensland. He has contributed to two other Society books, *Australia—Journey Through a Timeless Land*, and *Mississippi—River of History*. He is a graduate of the University of Queensland and has extensively photographed the northeastern tropics of Australia.

ACKNOWLEDGMENTS

We would like to thank the following people for their assistance in planning our journeys: Heike Lindenberg, Rovos Rail; Thomas Gainnini, Sierra Madre Express; Fiona Strang, Royal Scotsman; Missy Parella, Hawkins and Widness, U.S. representatives for Eastern & Oriental Express; and Sophie Dent, Indian Pacific Railroad. We would also like to thank Aubrey and Emma Cooper, Phyllis Cooper, Les and Eudice Daly, Bruce Davidson, Martie Van Eysson, Glenn Hall, Mark Hockenberry, Meg Quinn, and Rohan Vos.

INDEX

Boldface indicates illustrations.

WORLD'S GREAT TRAIN JOURNEYS
Adventure, Romance, and a Kangaroo or Two

Published by the National Geographic Society
John M. Fahey, Jr., *President and Chief Executive Officer*
Gilbert M. Grosvenor, *Chairman of the Board*
Nina D. Hoffman, *Executive Vice President*

Prepared by the Book Division
Kevin Mulroy, *Vice President and Editor-in-Chief*
Charles Kogod, *Illustrations Director*
Marianne R. Koszorus, *Design Director*
Alex Novak, *Managing Editor*

Staff for this Book
Melissa G. Ryan, *Project Editor and Illustrations Editor*
Rebecca Lescaze, *Text Editor*
Lyle Rosbotham, *Art Director*
Anne E. Withers, *Researcher*
Molly Roberts, *Photo Researcher*
Carl Mehler, *Director of Maps*
Matt Chwastyk, *Map Research and Production*
R. Gary Colbert, *Production Director*
Richard S. Wain, *Production Project Manager*
Janet A. Dustin, *Illustrations Assistant*
Deborah H. Patton, *Indexer*

Manufacturing and Quality Control
Christopher A. Liedel, *Chief Financial Officer*
Phillip L. Schlosser, *Managing Director*
John T. Dunn, *Technical Director*
Vincent P. Ryan, *Manager*

Library of Congress Cataloging-in-Publication Data

World's Great Train Journeys : adventure, romance, and
a kangaroo or two.
    p.cm.
    ISBN 0-7922-8028-8 (regular)—ISBN 0-7922-8029-6 (deluxe)
    1. Railroad travel. 2. Railroad travel—Pictorial works. I. National
Geographic Society. Book Division. II. National geographic.

G151 .W655 2002
910.4—dc21
                                        2002019171

One of the world's largest nonprofit scientific and educational organizations, the National Geographic Society was founded in 1888 "for the increase and diffusion of geographic knowledge." Fulfilling this mission, the Society educates and inspires millions every day through its magazines, books, television programs, videos, maps and atlases, research grants, the National Geographic Bee, teacher workshops, and innovative classroom materials. The Society is supported through membership dues, charitable gifts, and income from the sale of its educational products. This support is vital to National Geographic's mission to increase global understanding and promote conservation of our planet through exploration, research, and education.

For more information, please call 1-800-NGS LINE (647-5463) or write to the following address:

National Geographic Society
1145 17th Street N.W.
Washington, D.C. 20036-4688 U.S.A.

Visit the Society's Web site at www.nationalgeographic.com.

Composition for this book by the National Geographic Society Book Division. Printed and bound by R.R. Donnelley & Sons, Willard, Ohio. Color separations by Quad Graphics, Martinsburg, West Virginia. Dust jacket printed by Miken Companies, Inc., Cheektowaga, New York.